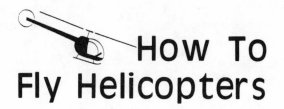

How To
Fly Helicopters

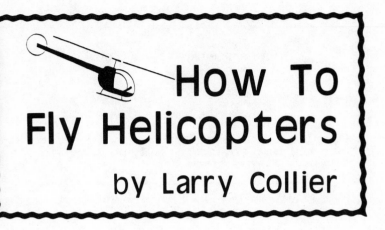

How To Fly Helicopters

by Larry Collier

MODERN AVIATION SERIES

TAB BOOKS

BLUE RIDGE SUMMIT, PA. 17214

FIRST EDITION

FIRST PRINTING—FEBRUARY 1979

Copyright © 1979 by TAB BOOKS

Printed in the United States of America

Library of Congress Cataloging in Publication Data

Collier, Larry.
    How to fly helicopters.

    Includes index.
    1. Helicopters—Piloting. I. Title.
TL716.5.C64   629.132′525   78-21015
ISBN 0-8306-9840-X
ISBN 0-8306-2264-0 pbk.

CONTENTS

1 Where It All Began 7

2 Aerodynamics 31

3 Aerodynamics of Flight 41

4 Flight Controls 55

5 Systems & Components 67

6 Flight Maneuvers: The Takeoff 77

7 Flight Maneuvers: The Hover 91

8 Flight Maneuvers: Preliminaries 103

9 Flight Maneuvers: Approach & Landing 113

10 Autorotations 125

11 Practice Maneuvers 135

12 Emergency Procedures 143

13   Special Operations 153

14   Introduction to the Helicopter Flight Manual........................169

15   Weight & Balance 181

Glossary 193

Index..207

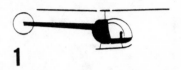

1

WHERE IT ALL BEGAN

The history of rotary-wing is a long and complex one. Its beginning is colored with uncertainty. Which came first, fixed-wing craft or rotorcraft? That question is as controversial as asking, "Which came first, the chicken or the egg?"

According to myth and legend , as far back as 3000 B.C., a Persian monarch harnessed a flock of trained eagles as a means of becoming airborne.

Early Greek mythology tells how an architect, Daedalus, and his son, Icarus, attempted to escape from the island of Crete by the use of wax wings. On jumping from a high mountain, Icarus was so struck by the beauty of flight that he forgot about escape and soared higher and higher. He ultimately soared too high, and the sun's rays melted the wax, causing the first known case of aerial structural failure from material fatigue.

For the first known document concerning rotary-wing flight, look to the great Taoist and Alchemist Ko Hung in the Fourth Century A.D. In the *Pao Phu Tau*, Ko Hung said that some had made "flying cars" from wood of the inner parts of the jujube tree. And, they used ox-leather fastened to returning blades so as to set the machine in motion. There's little doubt that this first plan for flight is the helicopter top, later known as the "Chinese Top."

The Chinese Top, dating back to the Fourth Century A.D.

Leonardo da Vinci spent some years trying to develop flying machines in Italy around 1485 A.D. He contributed to man's attempt to fly by sketching the most advanced plans of the period for an aircraft. He called it the "Aerial Screw," which was, in fact, a helicopter. Da Vinci's theory for "compressing" the air to obtain lift was similiar to that for today's rotorcraft.

Two Frenchmen, Launoy and Bienvenu, in 1784, demonstrated a scientific toy helicopter at the World's Fair in Paris. The toy helicopter, employing turkey feathers for rotor blades, rose to a height of about 70 feet. The machine created a startling amount of interest from representatives of various nations, who sent reports back to their respective countries. Inventors reasoned that if a man-made toy could be so developed, it should certainly be possible to build a larger model flying device capable of carrying men. If anything, it fired their imagination.

The famous English inventor, Sir George Cayley, demonstrated a helicopter in 1843 which featured lateral twin booms, each mounted with one set of rotors to provide lift. A small steam engine was housed in the fuselage and delivered power to the rotor system and twin, four-bladed propellers for horizontal propulsion. The twin-boom helicopter developed too little or no lift, however, it also served to stimulate the imagination of other inventors.

An Italian engineer Enrico Forlanini, constructed a steam-powered, contra-rotating, coaxial helicopter in the late 1870s. Its steam engine developed a total of 1/5 hp and weighed a hefty 6½ pounds. Reports say this machine climbed about 40 feet, remaining aloft for approximately 20 minutes.

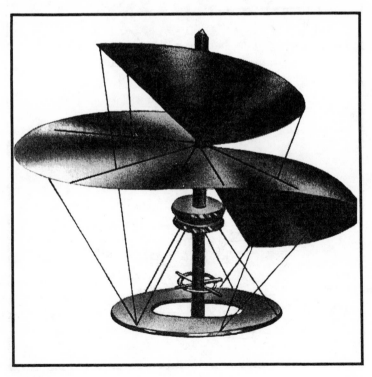

In about 1490, Leonardo da Vinci described a helicopter, based on the principle of the "Archimedian Screw."

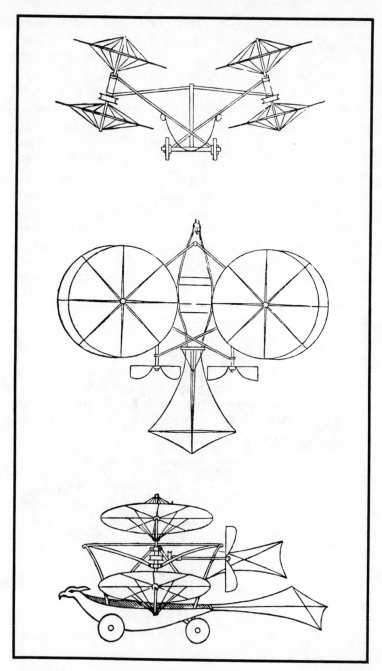

Sir George Cayley's three-view of his helicopter which was demonstrated in 1843. It was driven by a small steam engine.

By the beginning of the 20th Century, interest in rotary wing was stirring in such advanced countries as England, France, Germany, Italy, Spain, Russia and the United States. However, lacking an efficient powerplant, early inventors were limited. Another fact seemed fairly obvious: The turning of a single, overhead rotor system created forces that made the fuselage act erratic and, sometimes, uncontrollable. Early pioneers used either a coaxial, contra-rotating design or a twin rotor in which the rotors turned in opposite directions.

With the appearance of the internal combustion engine (gasoline), a major breakthrough was found for an efficient powerplant. It was the forerunner of successful flight with a high degree of efficiency (weight vs. horsepower). Engineers have since developed internal combustion engines that weigh less than one pound per horsepower.

In 1907, Paul Cornu, a Frenchman, constructed the first helicopter which showed signs of success. Cornu's copter had dual rotors, each about 20 feet in diameter, located fore and aft, and was powered by a 24-hp engine. Tilted vanes were used below the rotors for control purposes. Wide belts extended upward from the engine and outward to the rotors. These belts slipped considerably, but Cornu succeeded in rising vertically from the ground to a height of a few feet, thus becoming the first man to actually rise in true helicopter flight, even though his flight only lasted a matter of seconds.

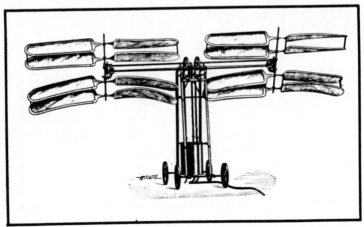

Enrico Forlanini's 1/5-hp, contra-rotating, coaxial helicopter of the late 1870s.

11

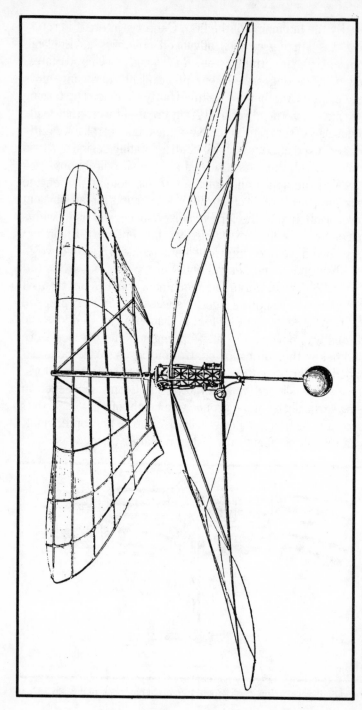

Castel Helicopter (1878).

Also in 1907, Louis Charles Brequet, another Frenchman, introduced a new design of the direct-lift aircraft, which he called a "helicoplane." It utilized four rotors and was a rather large machine. Each rotor consisted of four biplane blades. This copter attracted much attention. The Brequet-Richet No. 1 could become airborne, but had to be steadied by men holding it at all four corners. However, in 1908, the Brequet-Richet No. 2 flew skyward to a height of about 15 feet and forward some 60 feet. The second craft had only two rotors, mounted on fixed wings. The rotors had a fixed forward tilt. Although this machine was completely unstable and later crashed, it produced stimulation for fellow inventors.

Igor I. Sikorsky, later to become an outstanding figure in the industry, built two basic helicopter models: One in 1909 and the second in 1910. Although neither were considered successful, the second one was capable of lifting its own weight.

In 1916, following Sikorsky's experiments, Lt. Petroczy and Professor von Karmon of Austria constructed a con-

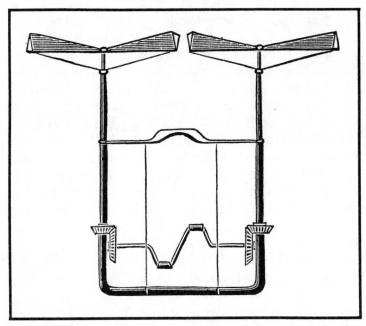

This machine was invented by Richard Owen in 1885. It provided for the pilot, and lifting screws were worked by foot-power.

trarotating, coaxial helicopter with three 40-hp engines that drove 20-foot rotors. This craft was used to serve as an observation platform. Three cables were attached to the craft in such a way that they would unreel from a ground control unit as the craft climbed vertically. Mounted above the rotating blades, a tub-type structure served as the observer's compartment. Before the cables were sufficiently taut on takeoff, the machine proved to have considerable instability. However, a number of flights were made to a satisfactory altitude for a duration of nearly an hour.

Henry Berliner, son of a Washington inventor, Emile, built and tested two entirely different helicopters in 1920-22. The first utilized a twin-rotor arrangement, with a 13-foot rotor diameter and vanes in the slipstream for flight control. His second copter was a dual-rotor design, powered by an 80-hp engine. Mounted on booms, the rotors extended from each side of the aircraft. Both of Berliner's machines were very unstable, but each flew several minutes on different occasions.

Dr. George de Bothezat, between 1920-23, built a helicopter under the auspices of the United States Signal Corps at McCook Field, Dayton, Ohio. It was the first helicopter designed and built under government contract. It consisted of four, six-bladed rotors, 25 feet in diameter. They were mounted at four points, similar to the Brequet design in 1907. The overall dimensions of the Bothezat aircraft were 65 feet in length and 65 feet in width. It weighed in at a clumsy 3400-pounds empty weight, but the inventor claimed it had a payload of 1000 pounds. Controls consisted of auxiliary propellers and variable-pitch main rotor blades. Bothezat's craft was one of the first to display encouraging stability and good control characteristics. Numerous flights were made, however these sorties had a duration of less than one minute, and the craft never rose more than six feet.

Also in the early 1920s, two helicopters were built by Etienne Dehmichen of France. A gas-filled balloon was utilized on the first. It was mounted longitudinally, with two lifting rotors located at front and rear. Though this machine lifted the weight of the machine and operator, it was found to be very unstable and uncontrollable. Four main rotors were used in

Curtiss-Bleeker.

the second Dehmichen craft that measured 21-25 feet in diameter. In addition, five small, horizontal props were incorporated. Two propellers for propulsion and one for steering were also used. Powered by a 120-hp engine, the craft incorporated 13 separate transmission systems. Even though more than 1000 flights of several minute durations were made in this helicopter, the complexity of the structure made it impractical.

Marquis de Pescara, a Spaniard, built several different man-carrying helicopters that performed well during the early and mid-1920s. The most successful one, a streamlined fuselage that resembled the body of a modern racing automobile. A coaxial, contra-rotating rotor system of a biplane-type was used, having a diameter of 21 feet. It was composed of six pairs of strutted blades, and the two rotor systems were arranged with one above the other. Horizontal flight was achieved by changing the pitch of the rotor blades during the cycle of rotation. Powered by a 120-hp Hispano-Suiza engine, this craft is reported to have demonstrated noteworthy flight characteristics.

A young, fixed-wing inventor, Juan de la Cierva, also a Spaniard, turned to exploring the rotary-wing field, wanting to develop a craft which could land at a low speed for maximum safety. Combining the features of the conventional airplane with that of the freely rotating, overhead rotor system, he developed a craft that was the forerunner of today's autogyro. Employing a conventional propeller in the nose of the aircraft, the autogyro used a large, overhead rotor system in lieu of fixed-wings to produce lift. Engine power driving the propeller created a forward thrust, with the resultant forward motion of the machine creating a favorable reaction on the rotor blades, causing them to "windmill," thus creating lift. A forward speed of about 30 mph would cause enough air to flow over the rotor blades to turn them at a sufficiently high rpm to support the aircraft in flight. This reaction is known "autorotation."

De la Cierva flew the English Channel in an autogyro in 1928. He took off from England and landed at Le Bourget Field, Paris, with an average speed of 100 mph. Much publicity was accorded this epic flight, because the machine proved

Langdon Helicopter.

extremely safe and foolproof, in that it could land at a low airspeed in a small area.

In 1930 the first helicopter incorporating a single, main rotor and a vertical tail rotor to compensate for torque was built by a Dutchman named von Baunhauer. A 200-hp engine drove the main rotor, and a separate 80-hp engine powered the tail rotor as a separate entity. Although this particular helicopter did fly, it was damaged before satisfactory tests could be completed.

Louis Charles Brequet, designer of the earlier and original four-rotor configuration, reappeared on the scene in 1935 with a coaxial-rotored aircraft, powered by a 350-hp engine. This new craft's arrangement demonstrated some promising characteristics, notably control and stability. However, it was extremely heavy, and there was a possibility of trouble from interference of the two rotors.

Many prominent, rotary-wing enthusiasts thought that the Brequet craft was the first successful helicopter ever built, although it was damaged beyond repair before the actual test data could be finished.

Germany's foremost designer of fighter aircraft during World War II, Heinrich Focke, in 1937, developed the Focke-Achgelis helicopter. Two large rotors were mounted on lateral booms, with each boom supporting its own rotor system. The main rotors, turning in opposite directions to compensate for torque were powered by a 160-hp, radial engine. This engine was cooled by a small, wooden prop, mounted on the nose-section of the engine. The machine weighed in at 2400 pounds and was controlled by changing the rotor-blade pitch.

Hanna Rasche, a woman test pilot, demonstrated its unique characteristics in the Deutschland Halle in Berlin. This auditorium was relatively small, measuring but 250 feet in length and only 100 feet wide. Retsch demonstrated hovering, 360-degree hovering turns, backward and sideward flight and remaining stationary over a fixed point.

The Focke FW-61 broke all existing international records in 1937 and 1939 and became recognized as the first practical, successful helicopter in the world. Some of its records were:

Pitcairn Autogyro.

Duration—1:20:49
Distance—143.069 miles in straight flight
Altitude—11,243 feet
Speed—76 mph

Resuming his study of rotary-winged craft, which he had started in 1909, Igor Sikorsky, in 1939, turned his efforts toward a single, main rotor and tail-rotor design. This new development called for coaxial rotor systems, with rotors turning in opposite directions to compensate for torque. The Sikorsky VS-300, on May 6, 1941, broke the world endurance record previously held by the Focke FW-61, by remaining aloft for 1:32:26, almost 12 minutes better than Focke's craft.

Design of the VS-300 included one main rotor, one tail rotor and two horizontal rotors mounted on booms extending laterally from the tail section. The main rotor produced lift, the tail rotor compensated for torque, and the horizontal rotors were used for directional control.

In 1941 the Flettner 282 made its flying debut. Like many of its predecessors, it had side-by-side, intermeshing rotors. Interesting features were the automatic control of rotor rpm by blade pitch changes and the automatic change to autorotative pitch in the event of engine failure. Anton Flettner could claim considerable success with his helicopters. The F1 was used operationally the next year.

During the period that Sikorsky was perfecting and leading the way with his helicopters, Arthur Young designed a copter for the Bell Aircraft Corporation, designated H-13. This machine had a semi-rigid rotor head, a two-bladed main rotor with stabilizer bar and a two-bladed tail rotor. It was a two-place, side-by-side craft, with a four-wheel landing gear. It was powered by a 178-hp Franklin engine.

A later model, the H-13D, incorporated a tail-skid, was powered by a 200-hp Franklin and mounted with suitable supports for two external litters. The H-13 was used for Army reconnaissance, artillery spotting, wire-laying and transportation. It made Army history with numerous, rapid evacuations of wounded troops from the battle fields in Korea.

Frank Piasecki first started his helicopter career with a small, one-place copter in 1943. It had a single, main rotor and

Louis Charles Brequet reappeared on the scene in 1935 with this coaxial-rotored craft, powered by a 350-hp engine.

an anti-torque tail rotor. Although it was only an experimental model, it did actually fly and launched Piasecki into his more famed models of tandem, dual design. These craft incorporated two, large, horizontal rotors, one mounted on the front and the other on the rear of the fuselage. Turning in opposite directions, the rotors thus eliminated torque reaction.

The tandem rotor design has a definite advantage in that the center of gravity (CG) travel load is not critical, since lifting rotors are mounted on the longitudinal axis of the fuselage at each end. Should a tendency toward a nose-heavy or tail-heavy condition develop, the rotor at that end would simply do more work, thus correcting the condition.

Piasecki's HRP-1 and HRP-2 were designed and developed in 1946. The HRP-2 had a stronger structure, but, otherwise, they were the same. Powered by a 600-hp Pratt & Whitney engine, the HRP-2 was a 10-placer, while the HRP-1 was powered by a 525-hp Continental and a 4-7 seater.

Later models by Piasecki were giants of the industry. Such models as the YH-16 and YH-21. The YH-21 was a 16-22 place, tandem rotored, single-engine rescue and utility craft, 20-feet-long and powered by a 1425-hp Wright engine. It had a 697-mile range, useful load of 2720 pounds, max forward speed of 120 mph and a 15,700-foot service ceiling. The YH-16 utilized a twin-engine, twin-rotor combination. The rotors, arranged in tandem, overlapping configuration, scribed overlapping arcs. An engine was located under each rotor and either engine could drive both rotors by means of an interconnected shaft. With rotors at each end of the 77-foot fuselage, this design permitted full use of the center portion of the fuselage for cargo or passengers and eliminated the balance problem encountered with single rotor-types. Cabin space available was 2250 cu. ft. for a disposable load of up to 40 persons, or 6000-8000 pounds. It was capable of flying 300 miles and returning to its point of origin with a crew of four and 27 passengers.

Stanley Hiller Jr. first entered the rotorcraft scene at the same time as Sikorsky and Bell, but his first, small, single-seated, coaxial craft, designated the XH-44, lacked stability. Engineering and production design for the Hiller 360 was completed in 1949. This model incorporated a "rotomatic"

Igor Sikorsky test hopping an early design.

Early model Hiller.

device, an airfoil surface with which the pilot aerodynamically controlled the main rotor system. Powered by a 178-hp engine, it was capable of carrying three people side-by-side and was, ultimately, accepted by the armed forces in 1951. Since this early-day craft, Hiller, like Sikorsky and Bell, has become a major success in the rotary-wing field.

Sikorsky Skycrane.

Still in wide use today is the Kaman K-1, with two, intermeshing rotors.

Also during 1950, the McDonnell Corporation, then of St. Louis, built a 10-passenger, dual-rotor, side-by-side, twin-engined machine. Entered in the Arctic Rescue Contest in that year, it proved to be a very worthy craft. McDonnell was the first to develop a small, single-place, jet helicopter designated the H-20, but better known as the "Little Henry."

During this period the Kaman Aircraft Corporation in Connecticut developed the HTK-1 helicopter. This machine was demonstrated, showing encouraging flight characteristics and employed servo flaps to tilt the rotor system, instead of control plates. Powered by a 240-hp, Lycoming engine, the craft had two, intermeshing rotors, each 40 feet in diameter. These rotors were located on lateral booms, giving it a max speed of 70 knots.

The rigid rotor Cheyenne takes off and lands vertically like a helicopter but flies with a speed of more than 250 mph.

The McCulloch MC-4 is a tandem aircraft, taking full advantage of the tandem configuration for a craft its size. The cockpit arrangement is for side-by-side, dual controls. It is 32 feet five inches long, with a height of nine feet three inches. It has a rotor diameter of 23 feet, max gross weight of 2300 pounds and a typical loading would be pilot, copilot and a passenger. It has a range of 200 miles at 75 mph, with 170 pounds of baggage or cargo. A 200-hp, six cylinder, air cooled engine is mounted horizontally to effect a horizontal output shaft. Equipped with a tricycle-type fixed gear, a full swiveling cantilever-type nose wheel is provided at the forward end of the craft.

The MC-4 is capable of a high speed at sea level of 100 mph, has a service ceiling of 10,000 feet, empty weight of 1600 pounds, a useful load of 700 pounds and a maximum rate of climb at sea level of 1000 fpm.

The Doman LZ-5 is a third generation model and features such key applications as a hingeless, four-bladed, oil lubricated rotor system that gives a minimum of vibration in the fuselage and controls. Body layout of the craft emphasizes an empty weight of 2860 pounds, useful load of 1559 pounds for a max gross of 4419. Service-wise, it's slanted for evacuation missions, frontline air observations and reconnaissance, wire-laying, supply and survey work. The machine is powered by a 400-hp Lycoming.

The Kellett Aircraft Corporation developed a large and powerful helicopter for the United States Air Force, designated XH-10. It has a twin, three-bladed, counter-rotating and intermeshing rotor. This type of rotor system eliminates the necessity for an anti-drag device, such as a tail rotor, leaving more power for direct lift. The configuration was first developed on the German Flettner craft, discussed earlier.

The XH-10 has a streamlined fuselage with tricycle gear, plexiglass-bubble nose and a horizontal stabilizer utilizing three vertical fins. A large cargo space inside the all-metal, semi-monocoque fuselage permits a wide range of uses. It has a large cargo door, with a hydraulic hoist in the cargo compartment to facilitate ground loading and airborne rescue.

This helicopter's 65-foot rotors are driven by two, 525-hp Continenta engines. It features such modernizations

The roll-out and first official flight of the armed version of the U.S. Army CH-47A Chinook helicopter in November 1965. The Chinook is a product of Boeing aircraft, Vertol Division.

as parking brakes, taxi brakes, full panel flight instruments, radio installation and a heating system. It can lift a gross weight of over 15,000 pounds while at a hover and cruise at a forward speed in excess of 120 mph. It can fly on one engine, at normal gross weight, at altitudes up to 4600 feet and has good autorotational characteristics.

Since World War II, development of the helicopter followed a predictable route, although frustratingly slow for those already convinced of the craft's potential. It was really the Korean Conflict that proved the helicopter to doubters: That it was an indispensable, multi-purpose tool, taking up where the fixed-wing airplane left off.

However, it was the Vietnam conflict that really started helicopters moving and firmly implanted them into our aviation society. For it was there in Vietnam that not only did the rotorcraft perform in an outstanding mode, likened to Korea, but carried it much further as those who flew the gunships can attest.

Hughes, Hiller, Enstrome, Bell, Sikorsky and many others are still paving the way, experimenting and making practical such items as fiberglass, polyresin coated rotor blades, Turbojets, etc., letting the rotorcraft mix well in a fixed-wing world.

2
AERODYNAMICS

Anything that flies; whether rotor, fixed wing, motorized or glider, does so through the use of airfoils. With them, an aircraft is able to get off the ground, maneuver through the air and land. Without them, flying would simply be an impossibility. Being so basic to flight, then, just what is an airfoil?

Airfoil

An airfoil is any device capable of producing lift. Almost everything is capable of producing lift to a certain degree, however, so almost everything can be called an airfoil. Take the ordinary, garden variety rock, for example. It can produce lift to a certain extent when moved fast enough through the air or the air moved fast enough over the rock.

Speaking specifically of aviation, an airfoil is described as, "any surface aerodynamically designed to produce a minimum of drag and a maximum of lift when air passes over it." Applied to fixed-wing aircraft, a common airfoil would be wing shaped. Applied to helicopters, it would be shaped like a rotor blade.

There are three main parts to an airfoil: leading edge, trailing edge and the camber. There is an imaginary straight line running from the leading edge to the trailing edge called the "chord line." The curve of the airfoil's surface above this chord line is called the "Upper Camber," and the lower curvature is the "Lower Camber."

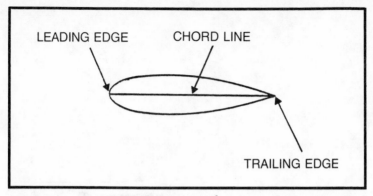

The chord line of an airfoil is the imaginary line joining the leading and trailing edges.

You'll find airfoils that are fat, thin, long, and short, but two that are basic to aviation are the "symmetrical" and "unsymmetrical." Most airplane wings are unsymmetrical, meaning the upper camber has more curvature than the lower camber. Currently, most helicopter rotor blades are symmetrical, in that the upper and lower cambers are of equal curvature.

Relative Wind

Before getting into such things as lift, weight, thrust and drag, take a look at a few things that affect the helicopter's blade; namely air movement, relative wind, pitch angle and angle of attack.

"Relative wind" is described as the direction of airflow in regards to the airfoil. Confusing? Not really. If the airfoil moves forward horizontally, the relative wind moves parallel to but in the opposite direction of that traveled by the airfoil. If the airfoil moves forward and upward, the relative wind moves parallel to, backward and downward. The relative wind always moves parallel to, but in the opposite direction of the airfoil's flight path.

In regards to helicopter rotor blades, relative wind is determined by three factors: rotation of the rotor blades through the air, flapping of the rotor blades (up and down movement) and the horizontal movement of the helicopter as a whole.

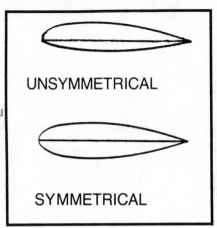

Symmetrical and unsymmetrical airfoils.

Blade Pitch Angle:

Using the horizontal plane of the main rotor hub as a base line, the blade's pitch angle is measured from the blade's chord line to the hub's base line. This angle is important, because it can be changed from inside the cockpit through the use of cyclic pitch control and the collective pitch control; two controls used to vary flight characteristics.

Even though the copter's body can turn on a horizontal plane, the blade's pitch angle will remain constant until changed manually by the pilot from inside the cockpit.

Angle of Attack

Similar to the pitch angle, in that angle of attack is also measured from the blade's chord line, it's different, in that it's measured not to the rotor hub line but to the relative wind plane. The angle of attack is determined also by the flight path of the helicopter, since relative wind runs parallel to it.

The angle of attack can be more than, equal to or less than the pitch angle. If you change the pitch angle of the blades, you

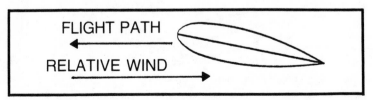

Relative wind is always parallel to and in the opposite direction to the flight path.

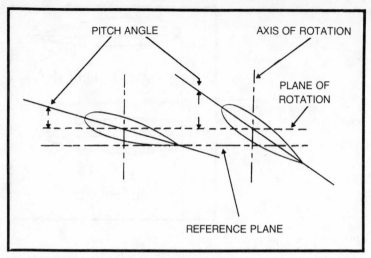

The pitch angle is the angle between the chord line and reference plane determined by the rotor hub or the plane of rotation.

also change the angle of attack, since you would be changing the blade's chord line in reference to the relative wind. However, the opposite isn't true; by changing the angle of attack, you're not necessarily changing the pitch angle of the blade. Remember, angle of attack is dependent on relative wind, and pitch angle is dependent on the rotor hub.

Lift

The values of pitch angle, angle of attack, relative wind, upper and lower cambers and chord lines combine to give you, among other things, varying degrees of "lift." How is lift derived from, and its relationship to, the above parts?

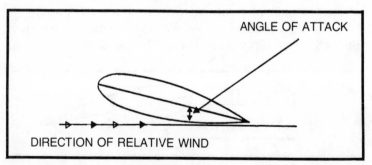

The angle of attack is the angle between the relative wind and the chord line.

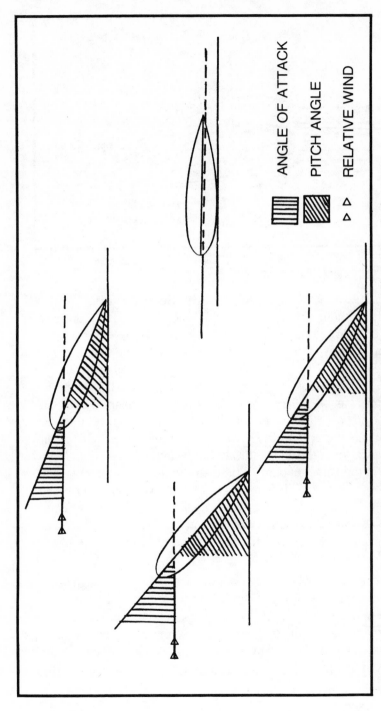

ANGLE OF ATTACK

PITCH ANGLE

△ ▷   RELATIVE WIND

The relationship between angle of attack and drag. As the angle of attack increases, lift and drag also increase.

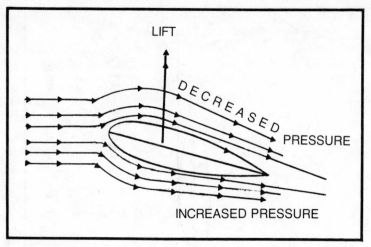

Lift is produced by a combination of decreased pressure above the airfoil and increased pressure below (bottom).

As basic as the airfoil is to flight, Bernoulli's Principle is to lift. Without either, flight couldn't be obtained. To capsulize Bernoulli's Principle, it says that as a liquid or gas (in our case, air) increases in velocity, the pressure of the liquid or gas decreases. Now, how does this apply to airfoils and lift?

Take a look at a normal airplane wing. You'll see that the upper camber is larger than the lower. This means that the air moving over the upper camber has farther to travel than the air moving around the lower camber. Even though the air moving over the upper surface has farther to travel, it must do it in the same amount of time as the air moving around the lower curvature. This means it has to move faster, increasing velocity and, according to Bernoulli, increasing its velocity over that of the lower camber, its pressure will decrease. This, in effect, makes the upper camber a low pressure area and the lower camber a high.

Since a low pressure is always a void that the high pressure system is trying to replace, there's vertical movement of the airfoil called "lift." Also, at the same time, air striking the lower camber builds up pressure even higher. The combination of the decreased pressure on the upper surface and the increased pressure on the lower surface results in an upward force.

If you increase the blade's pitch angle, the relative wind will strike the blade's leading edge lower down, thus giving the wind still farther to travel over the upper camber. And, having farther to travel, it must increase speed even more, causing an even lower pressure, which will, of course, result in more lift. So, by increasing the blade's pitch angle, you create lift.

It's true that a symmetrical airfoil produces symmetical airflow patterns above and below the airfoil at a zero angle of attack, and therefore zero lift. But at any positive angle of attack the airflow above the airfoil creates the familiar low pressure area as it does with asymmetrical airfoils.

Air Density & Lift

Although it can't be controlled as other factors, air density plays a great part in total lift. Take a look at the makeup of

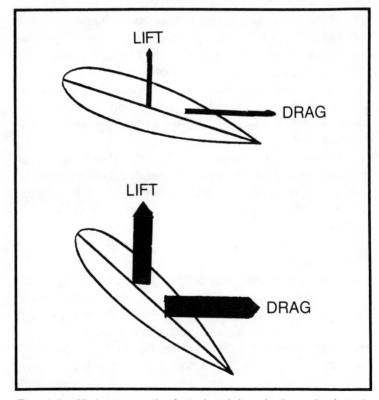

The relationship between angle of attack and drag. As the angle of attack increases, lift and drag also increase.

air density: temperature, humidity and pressure. Ideally, you would want a low temperature, low humidity and a high pressure. A combination of all three would give an airfoil its best lift.

With a "low temperature" the air is thick and compact. The lower the temperature, the more compact the air for creating lift. Just the reverse is true with high temperatures. The higher the temperature the thinner the air. Air that is heated expands. The higher the temperature the more the expansion, and the less air there is for creating lift. Remember, the lower the temperature, the more compact the air and the more air there is to move across the blade's surface to create lift.

"Dry" air is more dense than wet (humid) air. Therefore, the dryer it is the more compact, and the more air there is to move across the blade for increased lift. Water droplets in the air displace it, making it less dense. So, as humidity (water vapor in the atmosphere) goes up, lift comes down. Unfortunately, you seldom find dry air without it being hot; but again, we're talking about an ideal situation.

With a "high pressure," the air is compressed and compact, giving great volume to the air passing over the blade. However, with a low pressure, the air is expanded and thin, decreasing lift.

Capsulizing, thus far we have discussed two main factors in the creation of lift: blade pitch angle, which increases angle of attack, and air density, which increases the air's volume. There is, however, another very important item that also creates lift...Thrust.

Thrust

The faster a blade moves through the air, the higher the volume of air that moves over its surface. And, the higher the volume, like air density, the more lift produced. Although most helicopter pilots like to fly at a steady blade or rotor rpm, they can change its velocity, thus increasing or decreasing lift as desired. Just like in your automobile when you want to go faster, you simply "put your foot on the gas." It's similar with helicopters. If you want to increase blade rpm, you simply give it a little more go.

Another item not to be forgotten, since it has to do with rpm, is the blade's thickness. Using the same principle as with the air moving over the blade, you can readily see where the thicker the airfoil or blade, the more lift is obtained because the farther the air has to travel up and over.

Normally, you'll see larger helicopters, such as those used for heavy transport, using thick rotor blades. Thin bladed craft use a higher rpm than thick bladed ones.

Drag

At the same time the blade is producing lift, it's also creating another force called "drag." Drag is the term used for the force that opposes or resists the blade's movement through the air; you probably know it as the retarding force of inertia or "wind resistance."

Drag acts parallel to, but in the opposite direction of the blade's flight path. Also, you can say that it runs parallel to, and in the same direction as relative wind. It's this force that causes a reduction in rpm when changing to a higher pitch angle and/or a higher angle of attack. An increase in pitch angle or angle of attack not only produces an increase in lift but also an increase in drag.

Ever wonder why when you increase the power in your car, you increase in speed only to a certain extent, and to go any faster you have to again increase the power?

What you have is drag overcoming thrust. As your car accelerates so does drag. However, drag increases slower than thrust initially, then increases faster, until power or thrust is stalemated by resistances (drag).

Stall

When the blade's angle of attack increases to a certain point, the air can no longer flow smoothly over the top surface because of the required change in direction. At this point, where the air is breaking away from the upper camber, it's said to "burble." It's also at this point that lift is partially destroyed, and any farther increase in the angle of attack decreases the amount of lift proportionately. This loss of streamlined air flow results in a swirling, turbulent airflow and a large increase in the amount of drag. It's also at this point that the blade is said to be in a stalled condition.

If a stall is incurred, lift must be restored to the blades. This can be done is two ways or a combination of the two: increasing the rotor rpm, thus forcing the air to move back over the blade, destroying the burble and the stall; or the angle of attack must be decreased, enough so that the air will once again move over the blade. Since most pilots like to run at a steady rpm, it's only natural to correct a stalled condition by reducing the angle of attack with the cyclic stick, since changing the blade's pitch angle with the collective would also change the rpm setting.

Weight

The total weight of a helicopter (gross weight) is the first force that must be overcome if flight is to be obtained. Weight is overcome by the lift created by the main rotor blades. It's the force of gravity that works on a helicopter, acting downward toward the earth's center, regardless of the machine's flight path or attitude.

In a small craft, the thing to be most concerned with is not to exceed its maximum gross weight limitation. However, with the larger, more complex machines, another item must be reckoned with; that of balance. Not only must you keep the total weight at or below that specified, but you must also balance all of that weight within certain limits: Center of Gravity (c.g.). Too much weight concentrated in the front of the cabin area could cause drastic flight characteristics, as would too much in the rear area.

On some of the smaller helicopters, with side-by-side seating, even flight with one person creates an odd balancing situation when hovering. As you're taught to fly with an instructor, you get used to that weight balancing-out yours. However, when you solo for the first time, you might feel uncomfortable, because then the 165 pounds or so of the instructor are no longer present, causing a minor balancing problem.

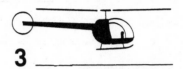

3

AERODYNAMICS OF FLIGHT

The basic ingredients of flight have been discussed in the preceding chapter. Now, put them together with different helicopter components and see how the craft aerodynamically lifts off, hovers, flys and lands.

Hovering Flight

In a no-wind condition hover, the helicopter's blade tip path is horizontal to, or parallel to the ground. Lift and thrust act straight up, and weight and drag act straight down. In other words, the sum of the lift and thrust forces equal and cancel out the forces of weight and drag. To hover, however, the craft must first get off the ground.

Vertical Flight

Vertical flight during a no-wind condition plays on the same basic forces as the hover. Lift and thrust forces act vertically upward, while weight and drag both act vertically downward. With vertical flight, however, the two groups are unequal. When lift and thrust equal weight and drag, the helicopter hovers. When lift and thrust are more than weight and drag, the machine rises vertically. If lift and thrust are less than weight and drag, the craft descends vertically.

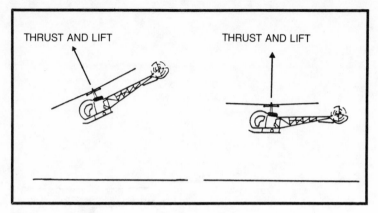

The total lift-thrust force acts perpendicular to the rotor disc or tip-path plane.

Forward Flight

Forward flight is accomplished when the rotor's tip path plane is tilted forward. The forward tilting motion thus tilts the total lift/thrust force forward of the vertical. The results of this motion divides the lift/thrust component into two forces: lift acting vertically upward and thrust acting horizontally in the direction of flight. The results of this combination is a lifting force which splits the two, called "resultant" lift.

In addition to the lift and thrust forces, there are again, weight and drag forces, plus any wind condition that's present. In straight-and-level, unaccelerated, forward flight, lift equals weight and thrust equals drag. If lift exceeds the weight component, the helicopter climbs in the forward flight attitude. If, on the other hand, lift is less than weight, the craft descends in the forward flight attitude. You can also say that if thrust is greater than drag, the machine will accelerate in the forward flight attitude. And, if thrust is less than drag, the helicopter decelerates or loses speed in the forward flight attitude.

Sideward Flight

Sideward flight is obtained by tilting the rotor head. This is accomplished through cyclic pitch control movement. Tilting the rotor head causes the total lift/thrust component to tilt sideways, this the vertical lift factor is still straight up, weight straight down, thrust moves sideward horizontally and drag acts in the opposite direction. Resultant lift; the splitting of lift/thrust forces, moves the helicopter to the side.

It can be readily seen that by tilting the rotor, flight can be made forward, sideward, rearward or in any direction you

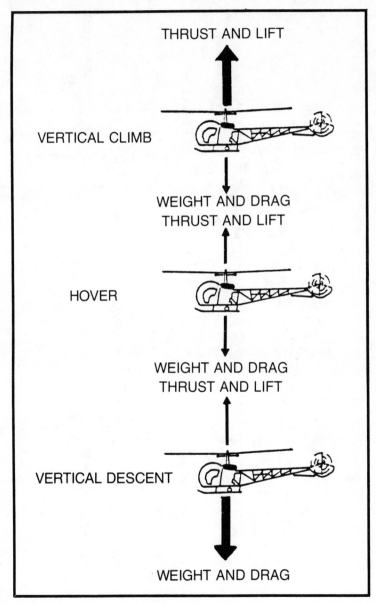

Forces acting on a helicopter during vertical climb, hover and vertical descent.

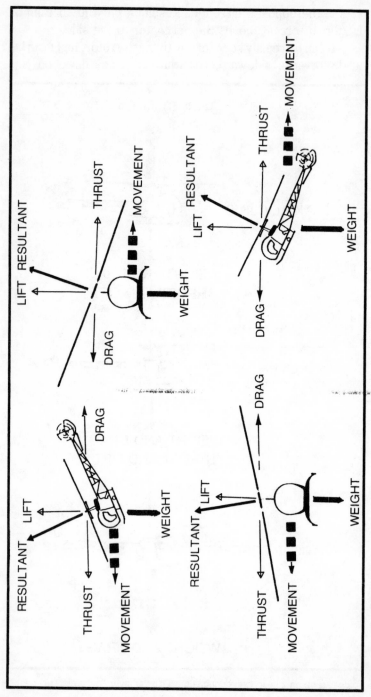

Forces effecting flight during forward, sideward and rearward movement.

desire to travel. As will be discussed in more detail later, this rotor head or hub tilting is accomplished by the pilot from inside the cockpit.

Torque

Another factor to be reckoned with and corrected for is "torque." Newton's Third Law Of Motion states, "To every action there is an equal and opposite reaction." Applied to helicopters, this simply means that the main rotor blades turn in one direction, normally counterclockwise, the helicopter fuselage tends to turn in the opposite direction, normally clockwise.

Since torque is the direct result of engine power supplied to the rotor blades, with the fuselage turning as a result of the engine's power, torque effect corresponds to engine power changes. If you add power, the torque factor increases; if you decrease power, the torque factor decreases.

Auxiliary Rotor(s)

If uncorrected, torque would cause an uncontrollable situation. It's most apparent at slow speed with high power output, such as in a hover, lift-off and during transitional flight. A force that compensates for torque and keeps the fuselage from turning in the direction of the rotor blade motion when powerless (autorotation) is produced from an auxiliary rotor,

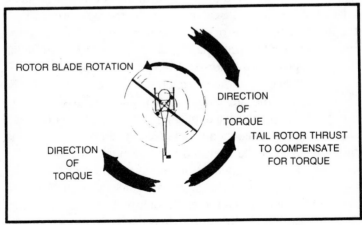

Tail (antitorque) rotor thrust compensates for the torque effect of the main rotor.

also known as a tail rotor or antitorque rotor, located at the end of the tail boom. It's simply placed vertically on the rear of the craft and produces thrust in the opposite direction of torque. Foot pedals (rudders) placed in the cockpit act with the similar action as rudders on fixed-wing aircraft, only controlling the auxiliary rotor's thrust, thus the pilot has a means of cancelling torque.

Gyroscopic Precession

The spinning main rotor of a helicopter acts like a gyroscope, in that is has the properties of gyroscopic action, one of which is precession. Gyroscopic precession is the resultant action (or deflection) of a spinning object when a force is applied to it. This action occurs approximately 90 degrees in the direction of rotation from the point where the force (deflection) is applied. It's through the use of this principle that the tip-path of the main rotors may be tilted from the horizontal.

By moving the cyclic pitch control in a two-bladed rotor system, the angle of attack of one rotor blade is increased, resulting in a greater lifting force being applied at this point in the horizontal plane of rotation. This same applied force simultaneously decreases the angle of attack on the other blade a like amount, thus decreasing the second blade's lifting force.

The blade with the increased angle of attack tends to rise higher in the plane, and the blade with the decreased angle of attack tends to lower. Because of the gyroscopic precession, the blades don't raise or lower to maximum deflection until reaching a point approximately 90 degrees after the initial deflection point in the horizontal plane of rotation.

In simplification, the retreating blade's angle of attack is increased and the advancing blade's angle of attack is decreased. This results in a tipping forward of the tip-path plane, since maximum deflection takes place 90 degrees later when the blades are at the rear and front respectively.

With a three-bladed rotor, the movement of the cyclic pitch control changes the angle of attack of each blade an appropriate amount, so the end result is the same: A tipping forward of the tip-path plane, when the maximum change in angle of attack is made, as each blade passes the same points at which the maximum increase and decrease are made for the two-bladed rotor.

As each of the three blades pass the 90 degree position on the left, the maximum increase in angle of attack occurs. As each blade passes the 90 degree position to the right, the maximum decreases in angle of attack occurs. Maximum deflection takes place 90 degrees later: Maximum upward deflection at the rear and maximum downward deflection at the front. The tip-path plane tips forward.

Dissymmetry of Lift

The area within the tip-path plane of the main rotor is known as the "disc area" or "rotor disc." When hovering in a no-wind condition, lift created by the rotor blades at all corresponding positions around the rotor disc is said to be equal. "Dissymmetry of lift," is created by horizontal flight or by wind during hovering flight and is the difference in lift that exists between the advancing blade of the disc area and the retreating blade arc half.

In a no-wind hovering situation, say the blade tips traveling the horizontal plane are moving at 400 mph. The speed of the relative wind at the blade tips can be said to be the same throughout the tip-path plane; or uniformly 400 mph throughout the complete circle. The speed of the relative wind at any specific point along the rotor blade will be the same throughout the tip-path plane. However, the speed is reduced as this point moves closer to the rotor hub, because the closer the point to the hub, the less speed is required to stay up with the blade tips.

As the helicopter moves into forward flight, the relative wind moving over each rotor blade becomes a combination of the rotational speed of the rotor and the forward movement of the craft. Looking down on the blade-path plane, at the 90 degree position on the right side, the advancing blade has a combined speed of the blade velocity, plus the speed of the helicopter. At the 90 degree position on the left side, the retreating blade speed is the blade velocity, less the speed of the helicopter. In other words, the relative wind is at a maximum at the 90 degree position on the right side and at a minimum at the 90 degree position on the left side.

Blade Flapping

Earlier, under "angle of attack" in Chapter Two, it was stated that for any given angle of attack, lift increases as the velocity of the airflow over the airfoil increases. It should be apparent that lift over the advancing half of the rotor disc will be greater than lift over the retreating half during horizontal flight or when hovering in a wind, unless some compensation is made. Equally apparent is the fact that the helicopter will roll to the left, unless some compensation is made.

With a three-bladed rotor system, the rotor blades are attached to the rotor hub by a horizontal hinge which permits the blades to move in a vertical plane, flapping up or down, as they rotate. In forward flight, assuming that the blade-pitch angle remains constant, the increased lift on the advancing blade will cause the blade to flap up, thus decreasing the angle of attack, because the relative wind will change from a horizontal direction to a more downward direction, thus decreasing some of its lift. At the same time, the decreased lift on the retreating blade will cause the blade to flap down, increasing the angle of attack, because the relative wind changes from a horizontal direction to more of an upward direction, thus increasing its lift component.

This combination of decreased angle of attack on the advancing blade and an increased angle of attack on the retreating blade, through this blade flapping motion, tends to equalize the lift over the two halves of the rotor disc.

In a two-bladed system, the blades flap as a unit. As the advancing blade flaps up, due to increased lift, the retreating blade flaps down, due to the decreased lift. Changes in the angle of attack on each blade by this flapping action tends to equalize lift over the two halves of the rotor disc.

Coning

Before takeoff, the rotor blades rotate in a plane nearly pependicular to the rotor mast. Centrifugal force is the major force acting on the blades. As a vertical takeoff is made, the additional force of lift takes place, acting upward and parallel to the mast. The result of these two forces makes the blades assume a conical path, instead of remaining in the plane perpendicular to the mast.

Coning, then, is the upward bending of the blades, caused by the combined forces of lift and centrifugal force. It results in blade bending in a semirigid rotor. In the case of an articulated rotor, the blades assume an upward angle throughout, by movement about "flapping hinges."

Axis of Rotation

There's an imaginary line about which the rotor rotates called the "axis of rotation." This axis is represented by an imaginary line drawn through the center of, and perpendicular to, the tip-path plane, and shouldn't be confused with the rotor mast. The only time the rotor axis and rotor mast coincide is when the axis of rotation is perpendicular to the rotor mast.

Coriolis Effect

In a three-bladed rotor system, when the rotor blades flap upward, the distance of the center of mass of the blades from their axis of rotation decreases. The distance of the center of mass from the axis of rotation (measured perpendicular to

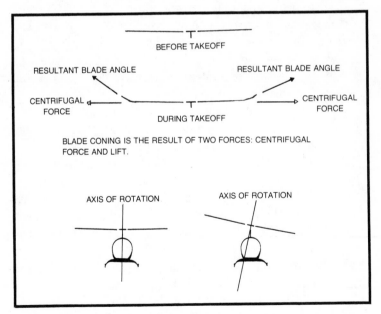

The "axis of rotation" is an imaginary line, perpendicular to the tip-path plane, around which the rotor moves.

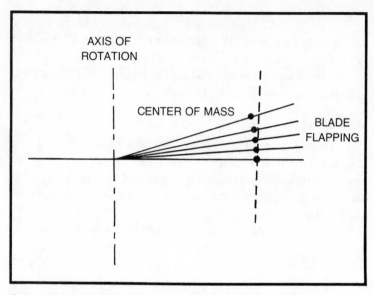

Coriolis effect takes place to compensate for the change in distance of the center of mass from the axis of rotation as the blades flap, changing blade speed.

the axis of rotation) times the rotational speed must always remain the same for a given rotor rpm.

Since this distance becomes shorter as the blades flap upward, the rotational speed must increase for the product of the two to remain the same. Conversely, when the blade flaps downward, the blade rotation must slow down, since the center of the mass is moved farther from the axis of rotation. This change in blade velocity in the plane of rotation causes a hunting action about the vertical (drag) hinge. This tendency of the blade to increase/decrease its speed is known as Coriolis Effect. The acceleration/deceleration is absorbed by dampers or the blade structure itself, depending on its design.

You might compare Coriolis Effect to a spinning ice skater. When the skater spins with arms extended, rotation slows down, because the center of mass moves farther from the axis of rotation. When the skater spins with arms held close to the body, the rotation speeds up, because the center of mass moves closer to the axis of rotation.

Two-bladed rotor systems aren't normally subject to Coriolis Effect to the degree of the three-bladed system, since the blades are generally "underslung" with respect to the rotor hub. The change in distance of the center of mass from the axis of rotation is small. What hunting action is present is absorbed through blade bending.

Translating Tendency (drift)

The entire helicopter has a tendency to move in the direction of tail rotor thrust, which would be to the right, when in a hover. This movement is often referred to as "drift." To counteract this drifting movement, the rotor mast in some helicopters is rigged slightly to the left side, so that the tip-path plane has a built-in tilt to the left, thus producing a small, sideward thrust. In other helicopters, drift is overcome by rigging the cyclic pitch system to give the required amount of tilt to the tip-path plane.

Ground Effect

When hovering close to the ground, a helicopter's rotor blades will be displacing air downward (pulling it through and shoving it down) through the disc area faster than it can escape from beneath the craft. This builds up a cushion of denser (more compact) air between the ground and the helicopter.

This cushion of compact air, referred to as "ground effect," aids in supporting the helicopter while in a hover. Ground effect is usually only effective at a height of ½ the diameter of the rotor disc. And, if the machine moves forward,

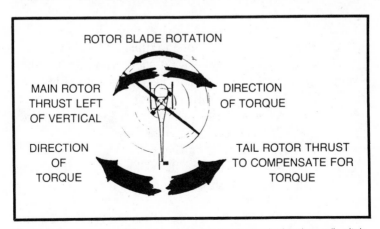

Tail rotor thrust causes drift and is compensated for by rigging the cyclic pitch system or mast to have a built-in tilt of the tip-path plane to the left.

normally faster than three to five mph, this effect is lost. Therefore, since the cushion is lost on helicopter movement, additional lift is required to keep from unexpectedly sinking back to terra firma.

Translational Lift

Another form of lift that enhances helicopter performance is created by its movement in any direction, except vertical. Sure, lift is lost when the copter moves out of its ground effect, but once it reaches approximately 15 mph in horizontal flight its rotor blades become more efficient, acting much as a fixed wing. The additional lift created at this speed and beyond is referred to as "effective translational lift" and is easily recognized by a sudden or marked increase in the craft's performance.

Since translational lift depends on airspeed rather than ground speed, the craft doesn't have to be moving to be affected. Translational lift will be present in a hover, if there's enough wind present (15 mph).

Transverse Airflow

With a helicopter in forward flight, air passing through the rear portion of the rotor arc has a higher downwash velocity than air passing through the forward portion. This increased downwash speed is caused primarily because the air passing through the rear portion has been accelerated for a longer time than the air passing through the forward part. In other words, the relative wind has a higher speed at the rear than the front.

This increase in relative wind speed and resultant lift, plus the gyroscopic precession, causes the rotor disc to tilt to the left side. According to the principle of gyroscopic precession, maximum deflection of the rotor blades occurs 90 degrees later in the direction of rotation.

This means simply that the rotor blades will reach maximum upward deflection on the right side and maximum downward deflection on the left side. The overall effect is a tendency for the helicopter to roll to the left. It's most noticeable on entry into effective translational lift where it can be accompanied by vibration.

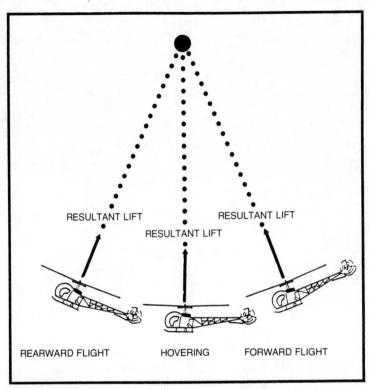

A helicopter acts much like a pendulum, since it's suspended from the rotor mast head; like a weight on the end of a string.

Pendular Action

Since the fuselage of the helicopter is suspended from a single point and has considerable mass, it acts much like a ball suspended from the end of a string. It's free to oscillate either longitudinally or laterally in the same way as the ball on the end of the string.

This pendular action can be exaggerated by over-controlling. Control forces (stick movement), therefore, should be decidedly moderate.

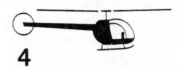

4

FLIGHT CONTROLS

There are basically four controls in a helicopter that you use during flight: Cyclic Pitch, Collective Pitch, Throttle and Antitorque.

With the use of these four controls, you can lift off, hover, transition, fly to your destination and land. By taking a look at their individual roles, as well as their integration into the total system, controls and the overall helicopter concept can better be understood.

Collective Pitch Control

The collective pitch lever, simply called the "Collective," is located on the left side of the pilot's seat in most models and is operated by the pilot's left hand. The collective moves up and down, with one end connected at the rear and, through a series of mechanical linkages, changes the pitch angle of the main rotor blades when moved up or down.

As collective is raised, there's a simultaneous, and equal, increase in the pitch angle of all the main rotor blades. And, as it's lowered, there's a simultaneous, and equal, decrease in main rotor blades pitch angle. The amount of lever movement determines the extent of pitch angle change.

As the rotor blades pitch angle changes, the angle of attack of each blade will also change. This change in the angle of attack will affect the blade's lift characteristics. As the angle of attack increases, drag and lift increase, however, rotor rpm decreases. As the angle of attack decreases, lift and drag decrease, but rotor rpm increases.

Since it's essential that rotor rpm remain constant, there must be some means of making a proportionate change in the power to compensate for the change in drag/rpm. This coordination of power with blade pitch angle is controlled through the collective's control cam linkage which automatically increases power when the collective is raised and decreases power when the collective is lowered.

The collective is the *primary* altitude control. Raising the collective increases the rotor's lift and, through the cam linkage with the throttle, increases engine power. The collective also is, therefore, the primary manifold pressure control.

Throttle Control

The throttle, often thought of as synonomous with the collective, is mounted on the forward end of the collective lever in the form of a twist-type grip on most helicopter models. The primary function of the throttle is to regulate rotor rpm directly and engine rpm indirectly.

In many smaller choppers there isn't any automatic syncronization of collective and rpm, or during an emergency with the more sophisticated, so it has to be done manually by twisting the throttle grip. Also, you may want to adjust or fine tune the rpm. Twisting the motorcycle-type grip outboard (clockwise) will increase rpm, and twisting inboard (counterclockwise) will decrease rpm.

The collective and throttle attachment work together, giving you the right blade pitch angle, manifold pressure (power) and rotor rpm. Since the collective is considered the primary control for manifold pressure and the throttle is considered the primary control for rotor rpm, they must work harmoniously together.

Remember, the collective also influences rotor rpm and the throttle also influences manifold pressure; each is considered to be a secondary control for each other's function. You must analyze both the tachometer (rpm indicator) as well as the manifold pressure gauge, which are usually housed in the

Collective and throttle (far left); Cyclic (center); and Antitorque (rudder) pedals (center left and left).

same unit for convenience. As a simplification, take a look at some sample problems that are common with this system and their solutions:

Problem: Manifold pressure low, rotor rpm low.
Solution: Increasing throttle will increase manifold pressure, and a higher rotor rpm will result.

Problem: Manifold pressure high, rotor rpm low.
Solution: Decreasing collective will reduce manifold pressure, decrease drag on the rotor, and a higher rpm will result.

Problem: Manifold pressure high, rotor rpm high.
Solution: Decreasing throttle reduces manifold pressure and results in a reduction of rotor rpm.

Problem: Manifold pressure low, rotor rpm high.
Solution: Increasing collective will increase manifold pressure, increase rotor drag, and a lower rotor rpm will result.

Flying a helicopter has often been compared to flying a heavy airplane at slow speeds. It takes time for corrections to be made; time between input of corrective measures on the controls and the time to helicopter response. It could possibly take as much as two seconds or more for the craft to respond to control input. This is one reason to avoid large adjustments. All corrections need to be accomplished through smooth pressure on the controls. Don't get anxious at not having a quick response and increase the input or put in another correction altogether.

Antitorque (rudder) Pedals

Thrust produced by the auxiliary (tail) rotor is governed by the position of the antitorque pedals. These pedals are linked to a pitch change mechanism in the tail rotor gear box and permits the pilot to increase or decrease the pitch of the tail rotor blades. The primary purpose of the tail rotor and its controls is to counteract the torque effect of the main rotor.

The tail rotor and its controls not only enable you to counteract the torque of the main rotor, but also to control the heading of the helicopter during a hover, hovering turns and

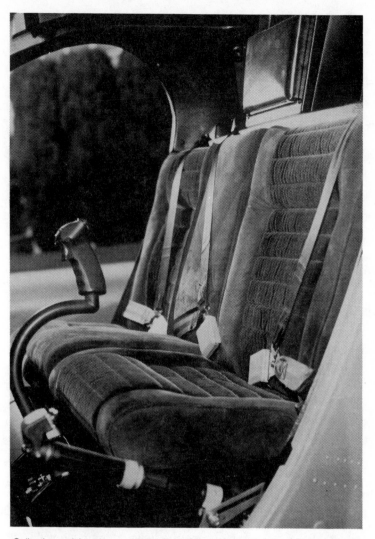

Collective and throttle are operated normally with pilot's left hand. Twist-grip type throttle and collective lever (lower).

hovering patterns. Understand that in forward flight, the rudder pedals are not used to control the heading of the craft, except during portions of crosswind takeoffs and approaches. They are, rather, used to compensate for torque; to put the helicopter in longitudinal trim so that coordination can be maintained. The cyclic control is used to change heading by making a coordinated turn to the desired direction.

For being so relatively simple, the development of an antitorque device puzzled the masters for many years. In any case, it takes no genius to understand the simplicity with which it works.

With the right pedal moved forward, the tail rotor either has a negative pitch angle or a small positive pitch angle. The farther forward the right pedal is pushed, the larger the negative pitch angle. The nearer the right pedal is to the neutral position, the more positive pitch angle the tail rotor will have. Somewhere in between, the tail rotor will have a zero pitch angle. As the left pedal is moved forward of the neutral position, the positive pitch angle of the tail rotor increases, until it becomes maximum with full forward displacement of the left pedal.

With a negative pitch angle, the tail rotor thrust is working in the same direction as torque reaction of the main rotor, and with a small positive pitch angle, the tail rotor doesn't produce enough thrust to overcome the torque effect of the main rotor during cruising flight. Therefore, if the right pedal is displaced forward of neutral during cruising flight, the tail rotor thrust will not overcome the torque effect, and the nose will yaw to the right.

The tail rotor will usually have a medium, positive pitch angle with the pedals in the neutral position. In medium positive pitch, the tail rotor thrust approximately equals the torque of the main rotor during cruising flight, so the helicopter is rigged to maintain a constant heading in level cruise flight.

With the left pedal in forward position, the tail rotor is in a high positive pitch position. In a high positive pitch position, tail rotor thrust exceeds that needed to overcome torque effect during cruising flight, so the helicopter's nose will yaw to the left.

This explanation is based on cruising power and airspeed. Since the amount of torque is dependent on the amount of engine power being supplied to the main rotor, the relative position of the pedals required to counteract torque will depend on the amount of power being used at any time. In general, the less power being used, the greater the forward displacement of the right pedal; the greater the power being used, the greater the forward displacement of the left pedal.

The maximum, positive pitch angle of the tail rotor is generally greater than the maximum negative pitch angle available. This is because the primary purpose of the tail rotor

Hughes 500 series antitorque (rotor) system.

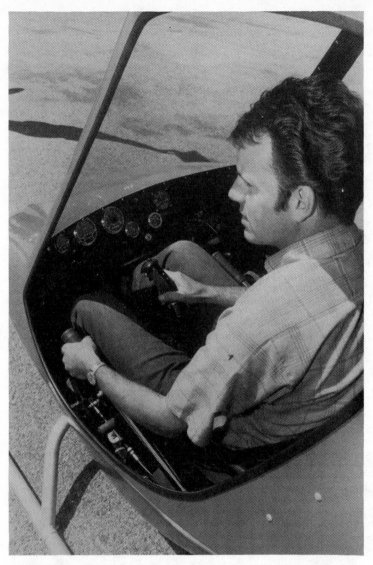

Cyclic pitch control between pilot's legs normally, and manipulated with pilot's right hand.

is to counteract the torque of the main rotor. The capability for tail rotors to produce thrust to the left (negative pitch angle) is necessary, because during autorotation, the drag of the transmission tends to yaw the nose to the left in the same direction that the main rotor is turning.

Cyclic Pitch Control

As discussed earlier, the at rest lift/thrust force is always perpendicular to the tip-path plane of the main rotor. When the tip-path plane is tilted away from the horizontal, the lift/thrust force is divided into two components: horizontal thrust and vertical lift. The purpose of the cyclic pitch control (cyclic) is to tilt the tip-path plane in the direction that horizontal movement is desired. The thrust component then pulls the helicopter in the direction of rotor tilt. The cyclic control has no effect on the magnitude of the total lift/thrust force, but merely changes the direction of this force, thus controlling the attitude and airspeed of the ship.

It sounds simple, because it is simple. The rotor disc tilts in the direction that pressure is applied to the cyclic. The rotor

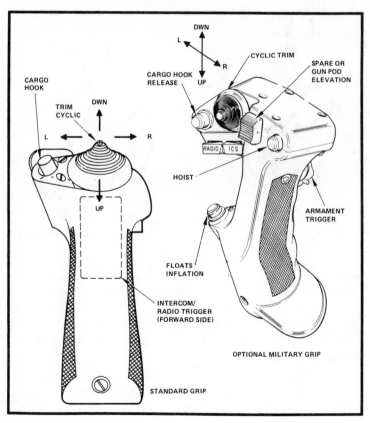

Cyclics range from a simple stick to this integrated cyclic grip.

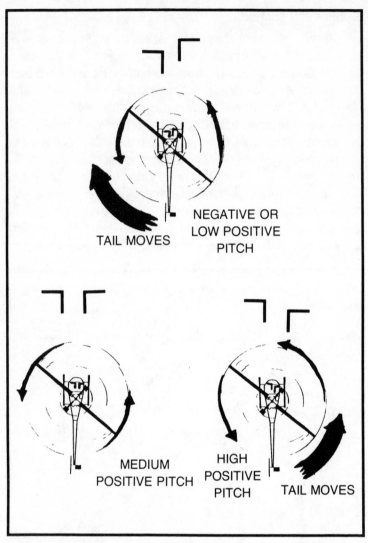

NEGATIVE OR LOW POSITIVE PITCH

TAIL MOVES

MEDIUM POSITIVE PITCH

HIGH POSITIVE PITCH

TAIL MOVES

Rudder pedal position in relation to tail rotor pitch and thrust, during cruise flight.

disc follows the input on the cyclic. If the cyclic is moved forward, the rotor disc tilts forward; if the cyclic is moved aft, the rotor disc tilts aft, and so on.

So that the rotor disc will always tilt in the direction the cyclic is displaced, the mechanical linkage between the cyclic and the rotor, through the "swash plate," must be such that the maximum downward deflection of the blades is reached in

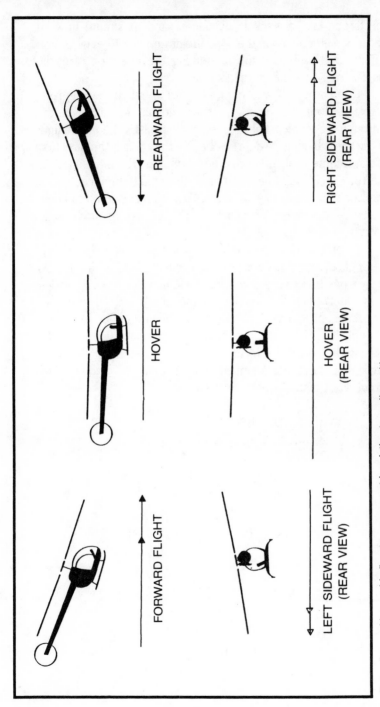

Rotor disc position and helicopter movement in relation to cyclic position.

the direction the stick is displaced; and maximum upward deflection is reached in the opposite direction. Otherwise, you would have a difficult job of relating the direction of cyclic displacement to the rotor disc tilt.

Remember, it was earlier stated about the 90 degrees between input and reaction. It also applies in this instance. Through mechanical linkage, which decreases the pitch angle of the rotor blades 90 degrees before they reach the direction of displacement of the cyclic; and increases the pitch angle of the rotor blades 90 degrees after they pass the direction of displacement of the cyclic stick. Any increase in pitch angle increases the angle of attack; any decrease in pitch angle decreases the angle of attack.

As an example, as the cyclic stick is displaced forward, the angle of attack is decreased as the rotor blades pass the 90 degree position to the pilot's right and increases as the blades pass the 90 degree position to the pilot's left. Because of gyroscopic precession, maximum downward deflection of the rotor blades is forward, and maximum upward deflection is aft, causing the rotor disc to tilt forward in the same direction as cyclic displacement. A similar analysis could be made for any direction of displacement of the cyclic.

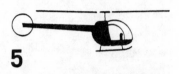

5

SYSTEMS AND COMPONENTS

In preceding chapters, we've discussed basic aerodynamics, aerodynamics of flight and flight controls. In this chapter, some of the other systems, components and their functions will be discussed to help familiarize you with the overall craft.

Transmission System

The transmission does just what its name implies: It transmits engine power to the main rotor, tail rotor, generator and other accessories. In a sense, it's what makes the machine go.

The engine must operate at a relatively high speed, while the main rotor turns at a much lower rpm. This speed reduction is accomplished through reduction gears in the transmission system.

A helicopter's reduction system is generally somewhere between 6:1-9:1. This simply means that, depending on which ratio is used, for every 6-9 engine rpm, the blades rotate one time. Using these ratios, then, it's easy to see that if the engine turns at 2700 rpm, for instance, the main rotor would turn up at 450 rpm at a 6:1 ratio and 300 rpm at a 9:1 reduction.

When the rotor tachometer needle and the engine tachometer needle are superimposed over each other in the same instrument unit, the ratio of the engine rpm to the rotor

Hughes 300 model power assembly.

rpm is the same as the gear reduction ratio. This single instrument unit, housing both engine and rotor rpm, makes for simple pilot readout and does away with superfluous instrument clutter.

Clutch

It's standard practice in the conventional, fixed-wing airplane to have the engine and the propeller permanently connected. Since the prop serves as a flywheel, there's no reason for the propeller to be at a standstill while the engine is running. With the helicopter, however, there's a different relationship between the engine and the rotor.

Since the helicopter's rotor weighs so much more than the prop of an airplane, it's necessary to have the rotor disconnect from the engine during start and warmup to relieve the load. It is, therefore, necessary to have a clutch between the engine and the rotor.

The clutch assembly allows the engine to be started and gradually assume the load of driving the heavy rotor system. The clutch doesn't necessarily provide disengagement of the engine from the rotor system for autorotation. This is accomplished through another device.

There are two basic clutch types: centrifugal and friction (belt). These two types of clutch operate differently but for the same purpose.

With the centrifugal clutch, contact between the inner and outer parts is made by spring-loaded clutch shoes. The inner portion of the clutch, the shoes, is rotated by the engine. The outer portion of the clutch, the drum, is connected to the main rotor through the transmission.

At low engine speeds, the clutch shoes are held out of contact with the clutch drum by the springs. As the engine speeds up, centrifugal force throws the clutch shoes outward until they contact the clutch drum. Motion is thus transmitted from the engine drive shaft to the input drive shaft of the transmission. The rotor starts to turn, slowly at first, but increases speed as friction develops sufficiently to drive the drum at engine rpm.

As the clutch becomes fully engaged, the rotor system is driven at the equivalent of engine rpm, and the rotor tachometer needle and engine tachometer needle join or "marry;" one needle superimposed over the other.

The rotor rpm equivalent to the engine rpm depends upon the gear reduction ratio between the engine and rotor system for that particular helicopter.

The friction or belt-driven system clutch is manually engaged by the pilot through a lever in the cockpit. Power from the engine drive shaft is transmitted to the transmission drive shaft by a series of friction discs or belts. With this type

Main rotor pitch links and pitch horn on R22. 1. Pitch link; 2. pitch horn; 3. teetering hinge, and 4. hub.

clutch, it's possible to start the engine and warm it up without engaging the rotors.

Freewheeling Unit

As previously discussed, the rotor system slowly engages and keeps up with engine rpm. When the engine slows below the equivalent of rotor rpm or stops altogether, the freewheeling unit-coupling automatically disconnects the rotor system from the engine. When the engine is disconnected from the rotor system through the automatic action of the freewheeling coupling, the transmission continues to rotate with the main rotor, thereby enabling the tail rotor to continue turning at its normal rate. This is important, because it allows the pilot to maintain directional control during autorotation.

Swash Plate Assembly

The swash plate consists of two primary elements through which the rotor mast passes: Stationary Star and Rotating Star.

The stationary star is a disc, linked to the cyclic pitch control. The disc is capable of tilting in any direction, but it doesn't rotate as the rotor turns. This non-rotating disc is attached by a bearing surface to a second disc, the rotating star, which turns with the rotor and is mechanically linked to the rotor blade pitch horns.

The rotor blade pitch horns are placed approximately 90 degrees ahead of, or behind the blade on which they control the pitch change. If this were not done, gyroscopic precession would cause the movement of the craft to be 90 degrees out of phase with the movement of the cyclic pitch stick. As an example, if the cyclic stick were moved to the right, the helicopter would move forward; if it were moved forward, the helicopter would move to the left, and so on, 90 degrees out of phase. Whether the pitch horns are ahead or behind, the blade will depend on the mechanical linkage arrangement between the cyclic stick, swash plate and pitch horns.

If pitch horns are 90 degrees ahead of the blade, pitch decrease of the blades take place as the horns pass the direc-

Top view rotorhead Hughes 500 series shows blade fairings.

tion the cyclic stick is displaced. Blade pitch increase takes place as the horns pass the direction opposite to the displacement of the stick. If the horns are 90 degrees behind the blades, pitch decrease will take place as the horns pass the direction opposite to the displacement of the cyclic. Blade pitch increase takes place as the horns pass the direction of displacement.

In either case, however, blade pitch decrease takes place 90 degrees ahead of cyclic stick position, and blade pitch increase takes place 90 degrees after passing the cyclic stick position. Thus, maximum downward deflection of the rotor blades occurs in the same direction as cyclic stick displacement, and maximum upward deflection occurs in the opposite direction.

In other words, when the cyclic stick is displaced forward, the swash plate's non-rotating disc tilts forward, and the swash plate's rotating disc follows this forward tilt. Since the mechanical linkage from the rotating disc to the rotor blades' pitch horns is 90 degrees ahead or behind the cyclic pitch change, the pitch angle is decreased as the rotor blades pass 90 degrees to the pilot's right and increased as the rotor blades pass 90 degrees to the pilot's left. Because of gyroscopic precession, maximum blade deflection occurs 90 degrees later in the cycle of motion. Thus, maximum downward deflection is forward; in the same direciton as cyclic stick placement, and maximum upward deflection is aft; causing the rotor disc to tilt forward in the same direction as cyclic stick placement.

Main Rotor System

Fully articulated rotor systems generally consist of three or more rotor blades. In a fully articulated rotor system, each rotor blade is attached to the rotor hub by a horizontal hinge, called the "flapping hinge," which permits the blades to flap up or down. Each blade can move up or down independently of the others. The flapping hinge can be located at varying distances from the rotor hub, and there can be more than one. The position is chosen by each manufacturer, primarily with regard to stability and control.

Scorpion Too antitorque rotor drive belt.

Each rotor blade is also attached to the hub by a vertical hinge, called a "drag" or lag hinge, which permits each blade, independently of the others, to move back and forth in the plane of the rotor disc. This forward and backward movement is called dragging, lead-drag or hunting. The location of this hinge is chosen with primary regard to controlling vibration. Dampers are normally associated with the fully articulated system to prevent excessive motion about the drag hinge.

Also, the blades can be "feathered" or rotated about their spanwise axis. Feathering means the automatic and periodic changing of the pitch angle of the rotor blades.

Semirigid rotor system's rotor blades are rigidly interconnected to the hub, but the hub is free to tilt and rock with respect to the rotor shaft. In this system, only two-bladed rotors are used. The rotor flaps as a unit, that is, as one blades flaps up, the other blade automatically flaps down an equal amount.

The hinge which permits the flapping or seesaw effect is called a "teetering" hinge. The rocking hinge that allows this teetering motion is perpendicular to the teetering hinge and parallel to the rotor blades. This hinge allows the head to rock in response to the tilting of the swash plate by the cyclic pitch control, thus changing the pitch angle an equal amount on each blade; decreasing it on one and increasing it on the other.

The rotor blades of a semirigid rotor system may or may not require drag hinges, depending on whether the system is "underslung." In an underslung system, the rotor blades lie in a plane below the plane containing the rotor hub pivot point. Because of coning, normal rotor operating rpm will place the center of mass of the rotor blades in approximately the same plane as the rotor hub pivot point. Consequently, the distance of the center of mass from the axis of rotation varies very little. Therefore, an underslung system is subject to coriolis effect, but to a lesser degree than a system that's not underslung. Drag hinges aren't needed, since the hunting action can be absorbed through blade bending.

Collective pitch control changes the pitch of each blade simultaneously and an equal amount, either increasing the pitch of both or decreasing the pitch of both.

In rigid rotor systems, the blades and mast are rigid with respect to each other. The blades can't flap or drag, but they can be feathered.

Because of their inflexibility, the rigid rotor system isn't one of the most popular. It's only been in the past few years that a great deal of progress has been made with their applications.

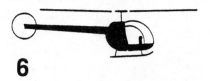

6

FLIGHT MANEUVERS: THE TAKEOFF

It should be obvious that the variable factors of wind, temperature, humidity, gross weight and structural differences of various helicopter models greatly affect their operation. Even when flying the same model, two flights are seldom exactly alike. Because of this variation, wind and density altitude, and flight characteristics must be adjusted accordingly.

It would be impossible, then, for a handbook to outline a specific nose attitude or power setting (these will be discussed in another chapter). The following maneuvers are accomplished at what can only be described as a normal day with the helicopter responding normally.

Although helicopter controls were discussed in an earlier chapter, a summary of their effects from the pilot's point of view will be helpful in understanding the various flying maneuvers presented in following chapters.

The "cyclic" or cyclic pitch control, tilts the rotor disc in the same direction as the cyclic is moved, and the helicopter moves in that direction. Thus, a backward displacement of the cyclic results in a nose-up tendency, followed by rearward flight; a sideward displacement results in a sideways tilt and sideways flight, etc. In normal, cruise flight, the cyclic is used much as is the control column or "joy stick" in a fixed-wing airplane. The main difference being, if a rearward displacement were held for long, the craft would, after climbing and losing airspeed, tend to fly backwards.

The "collective" or collective pitch control, in hovering flight is used to stabilize the helicopter's vertical movement. Raise the collective and the helicopter climbs; lower it and the craft descends. The primary effect of the collective is to control the engine's power; manifold pressure. If constant rotor rpm is maintained, the power will vary with the collective's position. Varying rpm is another collective function.

The twist-grip "throttle" control on the end of the collective is primarily used to control engine rpm. As stated above, the collective, to a certain degree, controls engine rpm, but the throttle is a considerable aid in maintaining rpm. It's often used by the pilot as a fine adjustment and can be used to obtain any desired rpm over the normal engine rpm range. Its second function is an alteration in power, and a small change can often result in a considerable change in boost.

The antitorque (rudder) pedals are used in powered flight to balance torque and to turn the craft in the yawing plane. As in an airplane, application of left rudder tends to yaw or turn the nose of the helicopter to the left and vice versa. In gliding flight (autorotation), rudder control is still available to maintain balanced flight or to turn.

The initial complexity of control coordination will be appreciated when it is stated that as one control is moved the other controls must generally be moved as well, especially in hovering maneuvers. As an example, consider the case of a helicopter about to move forward from a hover.

The stick is eased forward. The aircraft starts to move forward, but, because of the loss of the ground bubble, it also begins to sink. Up collective is applied to maintain the desired height, the throttle position must be altered to maintain rpm, which in turn changes torque. This means that the rudder pedal position must also be altered to maintain the desired heading. The change in rudder position affects the sideways drifting tendency, rpm and so on. When any forward speed builds up, the rotor disc will tend to flap backwards and more forward cyclic must be applied.

However, the control that consistently causes the most difficulty is the throttle. It's this twist-grip power control that

Bell Helicopter Textron's Model 222, the first U.S.-built commercial mid-size twin turbine helicopter.

has a direct or indirect action-reaction on all other controls. Increase or decrease power, and rudder, stick and collective adjustments must be made also.

Vertical Takeoff to a Hover

A vertical takeoff is a maneuver in which the helicopter is raised vertically from a spot on the ground to the normal hovering altitude, with a minimum of lateral and/or fore and aft movement.

To begin with, have the chopper headed into the wind. This is done to lessen complications when simplicity is the student's word. As your proficiency rises, this maneuver will be less of a problem. Place cyclic in a "neutral" position, and make sure the collective is in the full "down" position.

Make sure the craft is running in a warmed-up condition. You should now be sitting comfortably, with your feet on the pedals, right hand on the cyclic and left hand gripping the throttle control of the collective.

Open the throttle smoothly to acquire and maintain proper operating rpm. Raise the collective in a smooth, continuous movement, coordinating the throttle to maintain proper rpm. As the collective is increased and the craft becomes light on its skids (wheels or floats), torque will tend to cause the nose to swing to the right, unless you add a sufficient amount of left pedal pressure to maintain a constant heading.

As the helicopter becomes light on its skids, make the necessary control adjustments: cyclic corrections to ensure a level attitude on becoming airborne; pedal corrections to maintain heading; and collective corrections to ensure continuous vertical ascent to the desired hovering altitude.

When the desired hovering altitude has been reached, adjust throttle and collective as required to maintain rpm and altitude. Coordinate pedal changes with throttle and collective adjustments to maintain heading. Use the cyclic as necessary to maintain a constant position over the spot. Remember, the collective controls altitude, while the cyclic controls attitude and position.

Now, in a relatively stable position, check things out; engine and control operation, manifold pressure to hold hover,

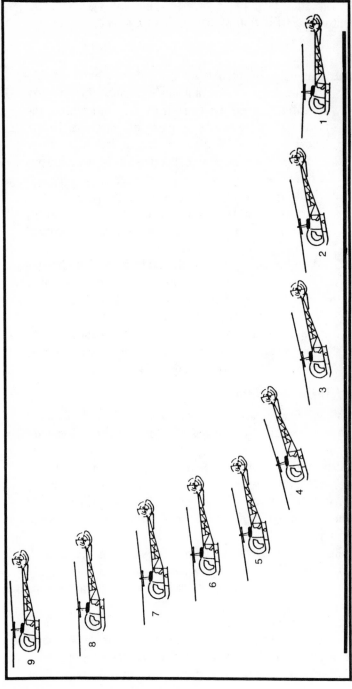

Normal takeoff from a hover. 1. Begin from normal hovering altitude. 2-4. Ease cyclic forward; increase collective to prevent settling. 5-7. Accelerate to normal climb speed, then raise nose to climbing attitude. 8-9. Make climb at normal climb airspeed.

81

and cyclic stick position. Cyclic position will vary with the amount and distribution of load and wind speed.

Errors

1. Failure to maintain level attitude upon becoming airborne. Any number of items can cause this, but to a greater degree it's caused by not anticipating the actions and reactions of elements present. Not to worry, as this will come with practice.

2. Pulling through on the collective after becoming airborne, causing the helicopter to gain too much altitude too quickly. This, in turn, will necessitate a comparatively large throttle and collective change, which will, in turn, produce even a greater degree of a problem, if not anticipated.

3. Overcontrolling the rudders, which not only changes the heading of the helicopter but also changes rpm, necessitating a constant throttle adjustment.

4. Reducing throttle too rapidly in situations where proper rpm has been exceeded, which usually means violent changes of heading to the left and loss of lift, resulting in loss of altitude.

Normal Takeoff From Hover

Takeoff from a hover is an orderly transition to forward flight and is executed to increase altitude safely and expediously.

After lifting the helicopter to a normal hover, check the engine and control operations. Note the cyclic stick position to determine if the copter is loaded properly. Check the manifold pressure required to hover to determine the amount of excess power available.

Make a 360 degree spot turn for clearing the area all around. Slowly, yet smoothly, ease the cyclic forward. Apply just enough forward cyclic to start the craft moving forward over the ground.

As the machine starts to move forward, increase collective as necessary to prevent settling when it departs ground effect. Adjust throttle to maintain rpm lost because of collective increase. The increase in power will, in turn, require an increase in left pedal to stay on heading. Keep a straight takeoff path throughout the maneuver, if necessary, picking two reference points.

As you accelerate to effective translational lift, and the helicopter begins to climb, the nose will begin to pitch up due to increased lift. Compensate for this nose-up tendency by adjusting collective to normal climb power, and apply enough forward cyclic to overcome nose pitching. Hold an altitude that will allow a smooth acceleration toward climbing airspeed and a commensurate gain in altitude so that the takeoff profile will not take you through any of the cross-hatched area or the height/velocity chart for that particular helicopter (see helicopter flight manual chapter). As airspeed increases, the streamlining of the fuselage will reduce engine torque effect, requiring a gradual reduction of left pedal pressure.

As the chopper continues to climb and airspeed approaches normal climb speed, apply rear cyclic pressure to raise the nose smoothly to the normal climb attitude. The normal climb attitude is approximately the attitude of the machine when it's sitting on level ground.

Errors

1. Failure to use sufficient collective to prevent settling between the time the helicopter leaves ground effect to when it picks up translational lift.
2. Adding power too rapidly at the beginning of the transition from hovering to forward flight without forward cyclic compensation, thus causing the craft to gain excessive altitude before acquiring airspeed.
3. Assuming an extreme nose-down attitude near the ground in the transition from hovering to forward flight.
4. Failure to maintain a straight flight track over the ground.
5. Failure to keep proper airspeed during the climb.
6. Failure to adjust the throttle to maintain proper rpm.

Note: If, for some reason, a takeoff can't be made into the wind, and a crosswind takeoff must be made, fly the helicopter in a slip during the early stages of the maneuver. To do this, the cyclic is held into the wind to maintain the selected ground track for takeoff, while the heading is kept straight along the takeoff path with rudder. Thus, the ground track and the fuselage are aligned with each other. In other words, the rotor is tilted into the wind to allow the aircraft to slip into the wind as much as the wind is pushing the copter sideways, effectively cancelling the wind's affect. To prevent the nose from turning in the direction of rotor tilt, you'll have to increase pedal pressure on the side opposite the rotor tilt. The stronger the crosswind, the greater the amount of rotor tilt and rudder pressure.

After gaining approximately 50 feet of altitude, establish a heading into the wind (crab), by coordinating a turn into the wind to maintain the desired ground track. The stronger the crosswind component, the more the chopper will have to be turned into the wind to maintain desired ground track. Once straight-and-level flight on the desired heading is reached, continue to use the rudders as necessary to compensate for torque to keep the craft in trim. Otherwise, there will be no other rudder correction for the wind in the crab attitude.

Running Takeoff

The running takeoff is used when conditions of load and/or density altitude prevent a sustained hover at normal hovering altitude. It's often referred to as a high-altitude takeoff. With insufficient power to hover, at least momentarily or at a very low altitude, a running takeoff is not advisable. No takeoff should be attempted if the helicopter can't be lifted off the ground momentarily at full power. There are two main reasons why this is always so:

1. If the helicopter can't hover, its performance is unpredictable.
2. If the helicopter can't be raised off the ground at all, sufficient power might not be available for a safe running takeoff.

A safe running takeoff can be accomplished only if ground area of sufficient length and smoothness is available and if no barriers exist in the flight path to interfere with a shallow climb.

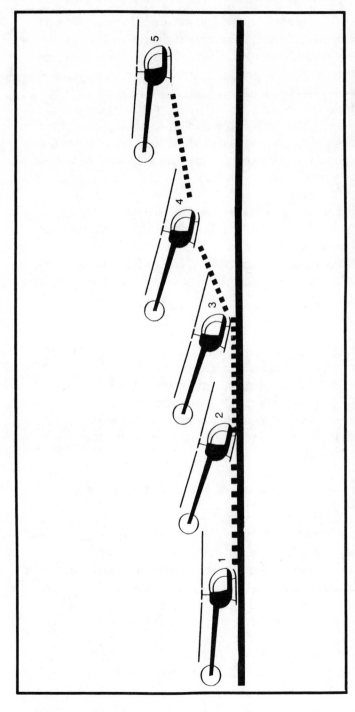

Running takeoff. 1-2 Adjust power for takeoff; usually one to two inches less than hovering position, for a gradual acceleration. 3. After translational lift is reached, ease cyclic rearward slightly to lift off. 4. Maintain 10-feet AGL or less until climb airspeed is reached. 5. Once climb airspeed is reached, adjust to climb attitude.

Head the copter directly into the wind. Increase throttle to obtain takeoff rpm. Hold cyclic slightly forward of the hovering "neutral" position. Raise collective slowly to one or two inches below that required to hover or until the craft starts to accelerate forward.

Maintain a straight ground track with both lateral cyclic and rudders for heading until a climb is established. As effective translational lift is attained, slight back pressure on the cyclic will take the helicopter into flight smoothly, in a level attitude, with little or no pitching.

Don't exceed 10-feet AGL, to allow airspeed to build to normal climb speed. Follow a climb profile that will take you through the clear area of the height/velocity curve for your particular helicopter.

During practice maneuvers, climb to 50-feet AGL, and then adjust power to normal climb and attitude to normal climb.

Errors

1. Failure to align heading and ground track to keep ground friction to a minimum.
2. Attempting to pull the helicopter off the ground before translational lift is obtained.
3. Lowering the nose too much after becoming airborne, resulting in the helicopter settling back to the ground.
4. Failure to remain below approximately 10-feet AGL, until airspeed approaches normal climb speed.

Maximum Performance Takeoff

A maximum performance takeoff is used to climb at a steep angle in order to clear barriers in the flight path. It can be used when taking off from small fields which are surrounded by high obstacles. Before attempting such a maneuver, though, thoroughly understand the capabilities and limitations of your equipment and the environment in which you're flying. Take into consideration the wind velocity, density altitude, gross weight of your machine and its CG location, as well as other factors affecting your technique and the performance characteristics of your craft.

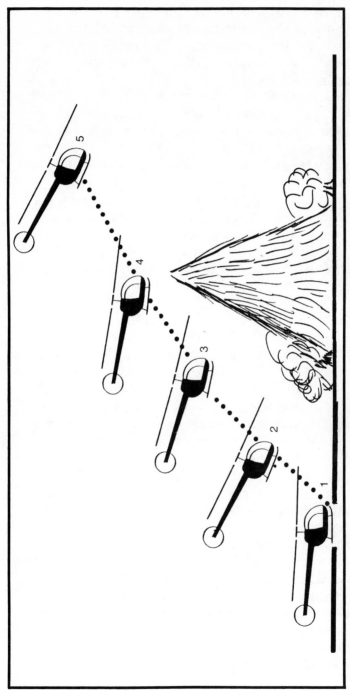

Maximum performance takeoff. 1. Increase: rpm to takeoff mode; collective until copter is light on skids. 2. Increase collective to maximum possible, without the loss of rpm. Add full throttle, as helicopter becomes airborne in the forward climbing attitude. 3-4. Maintain full power, without the loss of rpm. 5. Lower the nose to normal climb attitude to pick up climb speed, then adjust power to continue with normal climb.

To safely make such a takeoff, sufficient power to hover must be available to prevent the chopper from sinking back to the ground after becoming airborne. This maneuver will result in a steep climb, affording maximum altitude gain over a minimum distance forward.

The angle of climb for this type takeoff depends on existing conditions. The more critical these conditions—high density altitude, calm wind, etc.—the shallower the angle of climb. Use extreme caution in making a steep climb. If the airspeed is allowed to get too low, the craft could settle back to the ground.

Consult the height/velocity chart for your particular helicopter. An engine failure at low altitude and airspeed would place the helicopter in a dangerous position, requiring a high degree of skill in making a safe autorotative landing. It could be necessary to operate in the shaded area of the height/velocity chart during the beginning of this maneuver, when operating in a light or no-wind condition.

The angle of climb and resulting airspeed will be dictated by the proximity and height of obstacles to be cleared. You must be aware of the calculated risk involved when operating in the shaded area of the height/velocity chart.

The first step in a maximum performance takeoff should be to head into the wind, with the cyclic placed in what would normally be the neutral position for hovering. Check this position by hovering the helicopter momentarily prior to preparing to execute the maneuver.

Establish the proper rpm setting and apply sufficient collective to lighten the craft on its skids. Apply the maximum amount of collective that can be obtained without reducing rpm. Simultaneously add full throttle, and apply sufficient forward cyclic to establish a forward climbing attitude as the craft leaves the ground.

Use rudder pedals as necessary to maintain heading. Do not sacrifice rpm in order to obtain increased pitch on the rotor blades. If rpm starts to decrease under a full power condition, it can be regained only by reducing collective.

Use full power until the helicopter is clear of all obstacles, then a normal climb may be established and the power reduced.

Errors

1. Too much forward cyclic initially, allowed the nose to go down too far.
2. Failure to maintain maximum permissable rpm.
3. Movement of controls too abrupt.

7

FLIGHT MANEUVERS: THE HOVER

To a ground observer or even a passenger, hovering may look simple, because the pilot is apparently doing little and the helicopter is virtually motionless above the ground. However, since you've tried your hand at this maneuver or are about to, you should know that this isn't completely true: The pilot is maintaining position with the cyclic, keeping a fixed height with the collective, retaining the desired heading with rudder pedals and correcting any changes or rpm with the throttle.

The maneuver requires a high degree of concentration on your part as the pilot. Control corrections should be pressure rather than abrupt movements: A constant pressure on the desired rudder pedal will result in a smooth turn, while pronounced movements will tend to jerk the nose around causing other complications.

Smoothness on the controls can be accomplished by immediately making all corrections and not waiting out helicopter movement. Stopping and stabilizing the machine at a hover requires a number of small, pressure corrections to avoid overcontrolling. With practice, it becomes easier to anticipate the helicopter's movements.

The attitude of the copter determines its movements over the ground. While the attitude required to hover varies with the wind conditions and center of gravity (CG) locations, there's a particular attitude which can be found by experimentation that will keep the craft hovering over a selected point. After this attitude has been discovered, deviations can be easily noted and the necessary corrections made, often before the helicopter actually starts to move. This is really flying by the seat of your pants.

Coordination of all controls can't be overemphasized. Any change on one control will almost always require a correction on one or more of the other controls. Hovering can be accomplished in a precise manner by keeping in mind the small, smooth and coordinated control responses.

Errors

1. Tenseness which often causes late reactions to helicopter movements, or overreaction resulting in overcorrecting.
2. Failure to allow for lag in cyclic and collective which also leads to overcontrolling.
3. Confusing altitude changes for attitude changes, resulting in the use of improper cockpit controls.
4. Hovering too high; out of ground effect.
5. Hovering too low, resulting in occasional touchdown.

Hovering Turn

The hovering turn is a maneuver performed at hovering altitude. The nose of the helicopter is rotated either left or right, while maintaining position over a reference point on the ground. It requires the coordination of all flight controls and demands precision movement near the ground.

In calm air, a hovering turn is simple, but in a wind condition, the helicopter will be alternately moving forward, sideward, backward, sideward and then forward again, while turning on its axis. Also, the weathervaning stability of the copter is such that the initial turn out of the wind will be resisted, and on passing the downwind position the rate of turn will tend to speed up. Again, due to the wind, a fair amount of rudder will be necessary to make and control the turn, and this will have a considerable effect on the rpm.

Hovering in groun cushion during agricultural (aerial spraying/dusting) training.

Keeping the above factors in mind, the turn is accomplished with a feel for the helicopter's movements and by staying on top of the situation.

Start the maneuver from a normal hovering altitude, headed into the wind. Begin by applying rudder pressure smoothly in the direction you desire to turn.

When the nose begins to turn, and throughout the remainder of the turn, use cyclic to maintain position over the ground reference point. Use rudder pedals to maintain slow, constant rate of turn. Collective, along with the throttle, is used to maintain a constant altitude and rpm.

As the 180-degree position is approached in the turn, anticipate the use of a small amount of opposite rudder, as the tail of the helicopter swings from a position into the wind to one downwind. The machine will have a tendency to whip or increase its rate of turn as a result of the weathervaning tendency of the tail. Remember, the higher the wind, the greater will be this whipping action.

As you approach the desired heading for turn completion, apply opposite pedal pressure, as necessary to stop the turn on this heading.

During the hovering turn to the left, the rpm will decrease if power isn't reduced slightly. This is due to the amount of engine power that's being absorbed by the tail rotor, which is dependent upon the pitch angle at which the tail rotor blades are operating. Avoid making large corrections in rpm while turning, since the throttle adjustment will result in erratic nose movements due to torque changes.

Always make the first hovering turn to the left to determine the amount of left pedal available. If a 90-degree turn to the left can't be made, or if an unusual amount of pedal is required to complete a 45-degree hovering turn to the left, don't attempt a turn to the right, since sufficient left pedal might not be available to prevent an uncontrolled turn. Hover power requires a large amount of left pedal to maintain heading. Once the turn has started, sufficient left pedal in excess of this amount must be available to prevent an uncontrolled turn to the right.

Hovering turns should be avoided in winds strong enough to preclude sufficient back cyclic control to maintain the

Hughes 500 in hover.

helicopter on the selected ground reference point when headed downwind. Check the craft's flight manual for the manufacturer's recommendations on this limit.

Errors

1. Failure to maintain a slow, constant rate of turn.
2. Failure to maintain position over the reference point.
3. Failure to keep the rpm within normal operating ranges.
4. Failure to make the first turn to the left.
5. Failure to maintain a constant altitude.
6. Failure to apply rudder smoothly and cautiously.

Hovering Forward Flight

This maneuver is not so much a hover as it is keeping the helicopter from getting away from you, in what could be labelled as slow flight near the ground. Forward, hovering flight can generally be used to move the chopper to a specific area, unless strong winds prohibit crosswind or downwind hovering. A hovering turn is utilized to head the helicopter in the direction of the desired area, then forward flight at a slow speed is used to move to that area. During this maneuver, a constant, slow groundspeed, altitude and heading should be maintained. Care should be taken so as not to leave the ground-cushion effect.

Pick two reference points in front of and in line with the helicopter. These points can be any object that can be clearly seen. Keep them in line throughout the maneuver, since they guarantee a straight ground track while you're on the move.

Initiate the maneuver from a normal, hovering altitude by applying slight, forward pressure on the cyclic; only enough at first to start the helicopter moving.

As the craft begins to move, return the cyclic toward the neutral position to keep the groundspeed at a slow rate; no faster than normal walking pace. Ground effect will be retained at this speed, thus reducing the need for power and pedal corrections.

Keep a constant check on your reference points. Control groundspeed with the cyclic, a steady heading with the pedals,

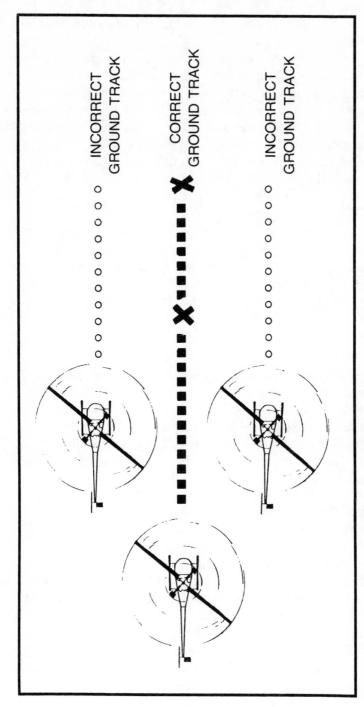

INCORRECT GROUND TRACK

CORRECT GROUND TRACK

INCORRECT GROUND TRACK

Use reference points to hold a proper ground track while in forward or rearward hovering flight.

a constant altitude with the collective and proper operating rpm with the throttle.

Upon reaching your desired area, apply gradual, rearward cyclic until the helicopter's forward movement stops. The cyclic must be returned to the neutral position when movement stops or rearward flight will begin. Forward movement can also be stopped by simply applying enough rearwind cyclic to level the helicopter and let it coast or drift to a stop. However the rearward cyclic pressure will require more lead time in this instance.

Errors

1. Erratic movement of the cyclic, resulting in overcontrolling and an uneven movement over the ground.
2. Failure to use proper rudder procedures, resulting in excessive nose movement.
3. Failure to maintain a hovering altitude.
4. Failure to maintain proper rpm.

Hover to Hover

This is a form of a longer-distance air taxi and is frequently used as a coordination exercise. It shouldn't be confused with a "quick-stop" (discussed later), which is an advanced exercise carried out more quickly and one in which the rotor is autorotating at one stage during the maneuver.

The transition to another area consists of a hover, then a gradual acceleration forward into the wind to about 60 mph, then a gradual return to a hover again. It's accomplished at a fixed altitude of about 20-feet AGL; higher than that of a normal hover.

The first part of the transition isn't too difficult. The technique is much like beginning a forward climb. Initiate forward pressure on the cyclic to get forward movement; slight up collective when ground resonance is lost, to hold altitude; rudder position to maintain heading; and an increase in throttle to regain rpm lost when collective was raised. You should now be in straight and level flight.

It's the slowing down upon reaching your objective that calls for careful attention. Ease back on the cyclic—this should be a very small movement—accompanied, or even preceded, by a downward movement on the collective. A corresponding change of a rudder pedal position is needed to maintain heading and a change of throttle to retain correct rpm.

When slowing down, translational lift will be lost. Power must again be increased, with a corresponding balancing of torque and rpm.

Errors

1. Failure to maintain altitude when entering translational lift.
2. Losing or gaining rpm.
3. Uncoordination on controls.
4. Failure to maintain altitude when leaving translational lift.
5. Moving too fast or slow between the two areas.

Hovering Sideward Flight

It could become necessary to move a helicopter to a specific area or position, when conditions make it impossible to use forward flight. In such a case, sideward flight may be a possible solution. It's also an excellent coordination maneuver. The primary objective is to maintain a constant groundspeed, altitude and heading.

Begin the maneuver by picking two reference points in a line running in the direction sideward flight is to be made. These two points will help you maintain proper ground tracking. Keep these reference points in line throughout the maneuver.

Initiate hovering sideward flight from a normal hovering altitude by applying sideward pressure on the cyclic in the direction you want to move.

As movement begins, return the cyclic toward the neutral position, but not all the way to neutral. Adjust to keep a slow groundspeed. Remember, ground effect will be retained, thus reducing the need for power or rudder corrections, at the speed of a walking person.

During the complete maneuver, maintain a constant groundspeed and ground track with the cyclic; a constant heading perpendicular to the proposed ground track with the rudder, a constant altitude with the collective; and proper operating rpm with the throttle.

Apply cyclic pressure in the opposite direction to that of the helicopter's movement and hold until the craft comes almost to a stop. As the motion ceases, the cyclic must be returned to the neutral position to prevent movement in the other direction. Sideward movement also can be stopped by simply applying enough opposite cyclic pressure to only level the helicopter. It will then drift to a stop.

Errors

1. Movement of the cyclic is erratic, resulting in over-control and uneven movement over the ground.
2. Failure to use proper rudder control, resulting in excessive nose movement.
3. Failure to maintain a hovering altitude.
4. Failure to maintain proper rpm.
5. Failure to make clearing turns prior to starting the maneuver.

Hovering Rearward Flight

This maneuver may be necessary to move the helicopter to a specific area when forward or sideward flight can't be used, as in backing into a parking pad surrounded by other craft.

As with previous maneuvers, pick out two reference points in front of, and in line with, the helicopter. These will help you in keeping a proper ground track. Keep these reference points in line throughout the flight.

Start rearwind flight from a normal hovering altitude by applying rearward pressure on the stick. After movement has started, position the cyclic to maintain a slow enough groundspeed that ground effect is maintained.

Keep a constant groundspeed with the cyclic; a constant heading with the rudder; a constant altitude with the collective; and proper rpm with the throttle.

To stop rearward movement, apply forward cyclic and hold until the helicopter almost stops. As the motion does

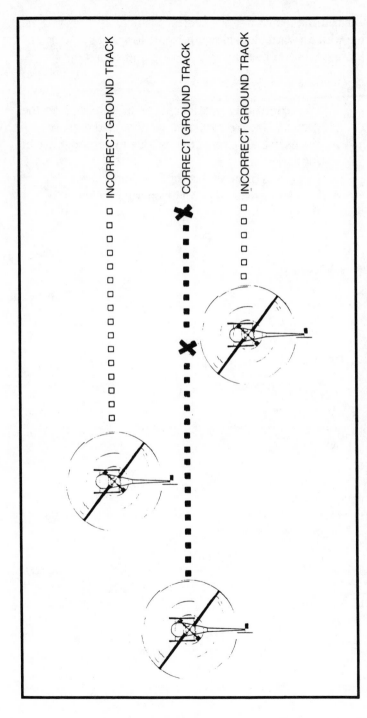

INCORRECT GROUND TRACK

CORRECT GROUND TRACK

INCORRECT GROUND TRACK

Use reference points in maintaining ground tracks. This includes sideward hovering flight, also.

stop, return the cyclic to the neutral position. Also, as was the case with forward and sideward flight, forward cyclic can be used to level the helicopter, letting it drift to a stop.

Errors

1. Overcontrolling and the uneven movement over the ground, due to erratic movement of the cyclic.
2. Excessive nose movements, due to improper use of rudder.
3. Failure to maintain hovering altitude.
4. Failure to maintain proper operating rpm.
5. Failure to make clearing turns before starting.

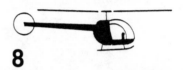

8

FLIGHT MANEUVERS: PRELIMINARIES

Flight in which a constant altitude and heading are mantained is considered "straight and level." The straight and level flight attitude is the attitude of the helicopter necessary to maintain straight and level flight. The level-flight attitude is the attitude of the helicopter necessary to maintain altitude.

Straight-And-Level

Airspeed is determined by the attitude of the helicopter. The attitude of the copter is controlled by the cyclic. Altitude is maintained by the use of the collective and throttle. In order to maintain forward flight, the rotor tip-path plane must be tilted forward to obtain the necessary horizontal thrust component from the main rotor. This will generally result in a nose-low attitude. The lower the nose, the greater the power required to maintain altitude and the higher the resulting airspeed. Conversely, the greater the power used, the lower the nose must be to maintain altitude.

When in straight and level flight, an increase in collective while holding airspeed constant with the cyclic causes the craft to climb; a decrease in collective while holding airspeed constant causes a descent. A correction on the collective requires a coordinated correction on the throttle in order to maintain a constant rpm; a correction on the rudder pedals to maintain

With wheels up for the first time Sikorsky's new advanced technology twin-turbine powered S-76 commercial helicopter maneuvers above the Florida countryside as part of its flight test and FAA certification program.

heading and longitudinal trim. Maintain coordinated flight without either slipping or skidding the helicopter.

To increase airspeed in straight and level flight, increase collective for more power, then gently apply forward pressure on the cyclic to maintain altitude. To decrease airspeed, decrease collective for reduced power, then add back pressure on the cyclic to maintain altitude.

As previously stated, expect a slight delay in control reaction from the time of correction input and the machine's response. The cyclic stick seems to be more prone to this delay than other controls. In making cyclic corrections to control the attitude or airspeed, take care not to overcontrol. Try to anticipate actual helicopter movement. If the nose of the craft rises above the level flight attitude, apply forward cyclic pressure to bring it down. If this correction is held too long, the nose will drop too low. Put in your correction, then wait for the resulting reaction. This is especially important, since the helicopter will continue to change attitude momentarily after you replace the controls to neutral, so anticipate such action

Hughes 500D over Southern California.

by bringing controls back to the neutral position just prior to reaching the desired attitude.

Most helicopters are inherently unstable. If gusts or turbulence cause the nose to drop, it will tend to continue dropping, instead of returning to a straight and level attitude. You must remain alert and fly the helicopter at all times.

Errors

1. Failure to trim properly.
2. Tending to hold pedal pressure and opposite cyclic (cross controlling).
3. Failure to hold best airspeed. Aft cyclic pressure dissipated airspeed without significant climb.
4. Failure to recognize proper control position for maintaining crab-type drift corrections.

Turns

This basic maneuver is used to change the heading of your craft. The aerodynamics of the turn have been discussed in previous chapters; lift components, vertical lift, resultant lift, load factors, etc. They should be thoroughly understood.

Before beginning, clear the area above, below and all around. It should be standard procedure with any maneuver. Enter the turn from straight and level flight. Apply sideward pressure on the cyclic in the direction of desired flight. This should be the only control movement necessary to start the turn.

(*Note:* Don't use the rudders to assist the turn. Use the pedals only to compensate for torque in keeping the helicopter in trim longitudinally.)

The more the cyclic is displaced, the steeper the resulting angle of bank. Therefore, adjust the cyclic to obtain, and maintain, the desired bank angle throughout the maneuver. Increase collective as necessary to maintain altitude, at the same time coordinating throttle to keep desired rpm. Increase left pedal pressure to counteract the added torque effect from the increased power. Depending on the angle of bank, swiftness of entry, power changes, etc., additional forward or rearward cyclic pressure may be necessary: forward pressure to maintain airspeed, or rearward pressure to keep the nose from falling out of the turn.

Recovery from the turn is the same as the entry, except the pressure on the cyclic is applied in reverse. Since the helicopter will continue to turn as long as it's in a bank, start the rollout before reaching the desired heading. Rollout lead-time is normally expressed in degrees, as you will usually be turning to headings. A rule-of-thumb is 5-10 degrees lead-time for angle of banks up to 30 degrees, and 10-15 degrees lead-time for more than 30.

Make climbing and descending turns the same as in straight and level, except that the helicopter will now be in a climbing or descending attitude. Establish entry by merely combining the techniques of both maneuvers; climb or descent entry and turn entry.

In a descending turn, however, an unusual feature occurs, especially noticeable to fixed-wing pilots. The craft can be turning to the left, but a considerable amount of right rudder is necessary to maintain balanced flight due to the low rotor torque.

A "skid" occurs when the helicopter slides sideways away from the center of the turn. It's caused by too much rudder pressure in the direction of the turn or too little in the direction opposite the turn in relation to the amount of collective (power) used. If the helicopter is forced to turn faster, with increased pedal pressure instead of increasing the degree of bank, it will skid sideways away from the center of the turn. Instead of flying in its normal, curved pattern, it will fly a straighter course. You could liken it to an automobile skid. If the steering wheel is the rudder, it's applying too much steering wheel for the speed or for the sharpness of the turn. Like the automobile, the helicopter will skid sideways in regards to the direction of wanted travel.

In a right, climbing turn, if insufficient left pedal is applied to compensate for increased torque effect, a skid will occur. In a left, climbing turn, if excessive left pedal is applied to compensate for increased torque effect, a skid will occur.

In a right, descending turn, if excessive right pedal is applied to compensate for decreased torque, a skid will occur.

In a left, descending turn, if insufficient right pedal is applied to compensate for the decreased torque effect, a skid will occur.

A skid can also occur when flying straight and level, if the nose of the helicopter is allowed to move sideways along the horizon. This condition occurs when improper pedal pressure is held to counteract torque, and the copter is held level with cyclic control.

A "slip" occurs when the helicopter slides sideways toward the center of the turn. It's caused by an insufficient amount of pedal in the direction of turn or too much in the direction opposite the turn, in relationship to the amount of collective or power used. In other words, if improper pedal pressure is held, keeping the nose from following the turn, the craft will slip sideways into (toward the center of) the turn.

In a right climbing turn, if excessive left pedal is applied to compensate for the increased torque effect, a slip occurs. In a left climbing turn, if insufficient left pedal is applied to compensate for the increased torque effect, a slip also occurs.

In a right descending turn, if insufficient right pedal is applied to compensate for the decreased torque effect, a slip will occur. In a left descending turn, if excessive right pedal is applied to compensate for the decreased torque effect, a slip also occurs.

A slip can also occur in straight and level flight if one side of the helicopter is low and the nose is held straight by rudder pressure. This technique is used to correct for a crosswind during an approach and during a takeoff when at a low altitude.

Errors

1. Failure to hold altitude when entering, during and exiting a turn.
2. Using unecessary pedal pressure for turns. Pedal pressure isn't necessary for small helicopters.

Normal Climb

Since entry into a climb from a hover has already been discussed, this section will be limited to climb entry from normal crusing flight.

Begin the maneuver by first applying rearward cyclic pressure to obtain an approximate climb attitude. Simultane-

Bell Helicopter's Model 206L LongRanger is shown in IFR configuration with vertical fins extending from horizontal stabilizer. The seven-place, light turbine LongRanger features Bell's exclusive Noda-Matic TM suspension system for outstanding ride smoothness.

ously, increase collective until climb manifold pressure is established. Adjust the throttle to obtain, and maintain, climb rpm. An increase in left rudder pressure also is necessary to compensate for the increase in torque. As you approach the desired climb airspeed, further adjustment of the cyclic is necessary to establish and hold this airspeed.

Throughout the maneuver, keep climb attitude and airspeed with cyclic, climb mainfold pressure and rpm with collective and throttle. Longitudinal trim and heading are maintained with the rudder pedals.

To level off from a climb, start adjusting to level flight attitude a few feet prior to reaching the desired altitude. The amount of lead you choose will depend on the rate of climb at the time of leveling-off. The higher the rate of climb, the more the lead. Apply forward cyclic to adjust and keep a level flight attitude which will be slightly nose low. Maintain climb power until airspeed approaches cruise airspeed, then lower the collective to obtain cruising manifold pressure. Make a throttle adjustment to cruising rpm, and you're there. Throughout the level-off, maintain longitudinal trim and a constant heading with the rudders.

Errors

1. Failure to hold proper manifold pressure.
2. Failure to hold proper airspeed.
3. Holding too much or too little left rudder.
4. In level off, decreasing power before lowering the nose to cruising attitude.

Normal Descent

To establish a normal descent from straight and level flight at cruising airspeed, lower collective to obtain proper manifold pressure, adjust throttle to maintain rpm, and increase right rudder pressure to maintain desired heading. If cruising airspeed is the same as, or slightly above descending airspeed, simultaneously apply the necessary cyclic stick pressure to obtain the approximate descending attitude. If cruising airspeed is well above descending airspeed, the level flight attitude may be maintained until the airspeed approaches descending airspeed, at which time the nose should be lowered to the descending attitude.

Throughout the maneuver, maintain descending attitude and airspeed with the cyclic control, descending manifold pressure and rpm with collective and throttle. Control heading with the rudders.

To level-off from the descent, lead the desired altitude by an amount that will depend on the rate of descent at the time of level-off. Remember, the higher the rate of descent, the greater the lead. At this point, increase collective to obtain cruising manifold pressure, adjust throttle to maintain proper rpm, increase left rudder pressure to maintain heading, and adjust cyclic to obtain cruising airspeed and the level flight attitude as the desired altitude is reached.

Errors

1. Failure to hold constant angle of descent.
2. Failure to adjust rudder pressures for power changes.

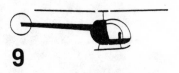

9
FLIGHT MANEUVERS: APPROACH AND LANDING

An approach is a transition maneuver which is flown from traffic pattern altitude, at cruising speed, to a normal hover. It is, basically, a power glide, made at an angle of descent matching the type of approach desired.

There are three basic approaches that you should be proficient in performing: normal, steep and shallow. You also should know how to analyze influential outside factors and how to plan an approach to fit any particular situation in which you find yourself.

Your choice of an approach is governed by the size of landing area, barriers in the approach path, type of ground surface, temperature, altitude, humidity (density altitude), wind direction, wind speed and the gross weight of your craft. Give a little tolerance for overshooting or undershooting a chosen landing spot, and in order to maintain a maximum safety margin in each type of approach, retain translational lift as long as practicable.

Evaluation of existing wind conditions must be made before initiating an approach. Although the approach is generally made into the wind, conditions can indicate the entry will have to be made from a downwind or crosswind position. The traffic pattern is generally flown at normal cruise airspeed. The velocity of the wind determines the airspeed that will be

The HueyCobra, designated AH-1G by the United States Army, is manufactured by Textron's Bell Helicopter Company in Fort Worth, Texas.

maintained after the approach is started. Increase airspeed in proportion to any increase in wind velocity. Keep the angle of descent constant, regardless of wind speed.

Crosswind approaches are made by crabbing or slipping or a combination of both. To make running landings in strong crosswinds, it may be necessary to touch down, initially, with the upwind skid (skid that's into the wind), to avoid drifting.

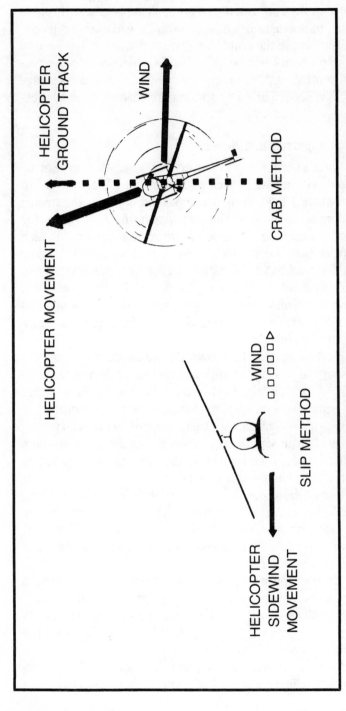

Slip method as compared to the crab method of wind drift correction. Slip method is normally used for close to the ground work, such as in takeoff, air taxi and landings; crab method is used in normal flight configuration.

Keep the rpm constant during all approaches. If rpm is allowed to fluctuate or change abruptly, variations or torque forces will cause the craft's fuselage to yaw around its vertical axis, and control will be difficult. To maintain proper directional control, make rpm changes and/or collective settings smoothly, accompanied by appropriate changes in pedal pressure.

Normal Approach to a Hover

Make a normal airport pattern entry at a 45-degree angle to the downwind leg in such a manner that the actual turn to the downwind leg will be accomplished opposite the middle one-third of the runway. The transition from the downwind leg to final approach can be made by two 90-degree turns in which a definite base leg is established or by a single 180-degree turn. Remember, at all times during this transition, keep sufficient altitude in case of engine failure. In such a case, you would want to make an autorotative landing into the wind. This fact will determine the point in the traffic pattern where a power reduction is made.

Start the approach by lowering the collective the amount necessary to descend at approximately a 12-degree angle on the final approach leg. As the collective is lowered, increase right pedal as necessary to compensate for the change in torque to maintain heading. Adjust throttle to maintain proper rpm. Hold attitude with cyclic control until the airspeed nears approach speed, then adjust with the cyclic to the attitude that will maintain this approach speed.

The angle of descent and rate of descent are primarily controlled by collective; the airspeed is primarily controlled by the cyclic; and heading on final with the rudders. However, only with coordination of all controls can the approach be made successfully.

Maintain approach airspeed until the point on the circuit is reached where, through evaluation of apparent ground speed, it's determined that forward airspeed must be progressively decreased to arrive at hovering altitude and an attitude at the landing spot with a zero ground speed.

As forward airspeed is gradually reduced by applying rearward cyclic, additional power through the collective must

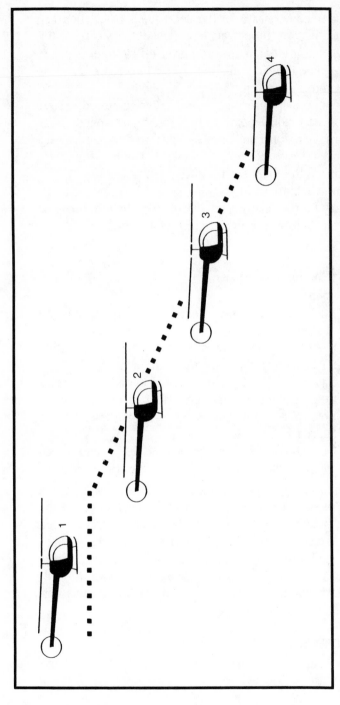

Normal approach to a hover: 1. Set to approach power and rpm. 2. Enter descent at proper airspeed, maintaining angle of descent with collective and airspeed with cyclic. 3. At approximately 50 ft AGL, progressively decrease ground speed to arrive at hover over selected spot. You'll have to increase collective as translational lift is lost to hold proper approach angle. 4. When approaching the hover, make sure your craft is level. Make final power adjustment and hover.

be applied to compensate for the decrease in translational lift and to maintain the proper angle of descent. As collective is increased, left rudder must be increased to keep heading; throttle adjusted to hold rpm; and cyclic coordinated to maintain the proper change in forward airspeed.

The approach is terminated at hovering altitude above your intended landing point with zero ground speed. Very little, if any, additional power is required to stop the forward movement and rate of descent if power has been properly applied during the final portion of the approach.

If the condition of the landing spot is unknown, the approach may be terminated just short of the spot so it can be checked out before moving forward for touchdown.

Errors

1. Failure to maintain proper rpm during the entire approach.
2. Improper use of the collective in controlling the rate of descent.
3. Failure to make rudder corrections to compensate for collective changes during the approach.
4. Failure to arrive at hovering altitude, hovering attitude and zero ground speed almost simultaneously.
5. Low rpm in transition to the hover at the end of the approach.
6. Using too much aft cyclic close to the ground, which could result in the tail rotor striking the ground.

(*Note*: During the early stages of a crosswind approach, a crab and/or slip may be used. During the final stages of the approach, beginning about 50-feet AGL, a slip should be used to align the fuselage with the ground track. The rotor is tilted into the wind with cyclic enough to cancel the wind drift. Heading is maintained along the ground track with the rudders. Use this technique on any type of crosswind approach; shallow, normal or steep.)

Steep Approach to a Hover

A steep approach is used primarily when obstacles in the approach path are too high to allow a normal approach. It will

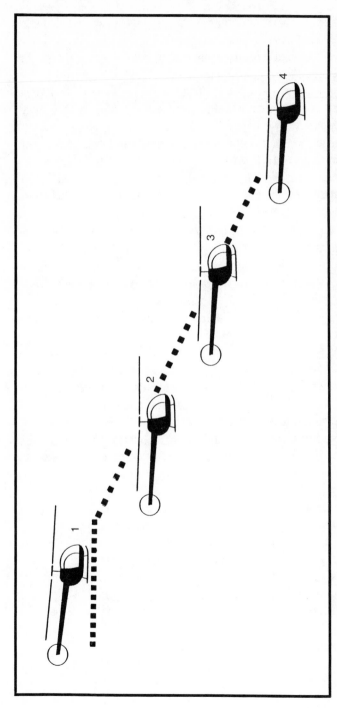

Steep approach to a hover: 1. Set to approach power and rpm. 2. Enter descent at proper airspeed, holding angle of descent with collective and airspeed with cyclic (unless manufacturer recommends otherwise), progressively decrease ground speed to arrive at hover over selected spot. 4. When approaching the hover, make sure the craft is level.

permit entry into most confined areas. Use an approach angle of 12-20 degrees.

Entry is made in the same manner as a normal approach, except that a greater reduction of collective is required at the beginning of the approach to start the descent. As collective is lowered, increase right rudder pressure to maintain heading, and adjust throttle to hold rpm.

As in the normal approach, the angle and rate of descent are primarily controlled by collective pitch, and the airspeed is primarily controlled by the cyclic. However only with the coordination of all controls can the approach be accomplished successfully.

Maintain approach airspeed until the point on the approach is reached where, through evaluation of apparent ground speed, it's determined that forward airspeed must be progressively decreased in order to arrive at hovering altitude at the intended landing spot with zero ground speed. This is very important, since a flare shouldn't be made near the ground due to the danger of the tail rotor striking.

As forward speed is gradually reduced by the application of rearward cyclic pressure, additional power from the collective must be applied to compensate for the decrease in translational lift and to maintain the proper angle of descent. As collective pitch is increased, left rudder pressure must be increased to maintain heading. Adjust throttle to keep proper rpm, and cyclic pitch is coordinated to control the change in forward airspeed.

Since the rate of descent on a steep approach is much higher than for normal approaches, the collective must be used much sooner at the bottom of the approach. The approach is terminated at hovering altitude above the intended landing point with zero ground speed. Very little, if any, additional power should be required to stop the forward movement and rate of descent of the helicopter if power has been properly applied during the final portion of the approach.

Errors

1. Failure to maintain proper rpm during the entire approach.

2. Improper use of collective in controlling the rate of descent.
3. Failure to make pedal corrections to compensate for collective pitch changes during the approach.
4. Slowing airspeed excessively in order to remain on the proper angle of descent.
5. Failure to arrive at hovering altitude, hovering attitude and zero ground speed almost simultaneously.
6. Low rpm in transition to the hover at the end of the approach.
7. Using too much rearward cyclic close to the ground, which could result in the tail rotor striking the ground.

Landing From a Hover

In Chapter Six, how to takeoff to a hover was discussed. Here's its sequel, how to land vertically from a hover.

From an already attained hover, begin your descent by applying a slow, but gradual, downward pressure on the collective. Maintain a constant rate of descent to the ground. As the skids come to within a few feet of the surface, ground cushion effect becomes very noticeable, and the helicopter tends to stop its descent altogether. At this point, it may be necessary to further decrease the collective in order to maintain the constant rate of descent.

When the skids touch the ground, lower the collective to the full down position, adjust the throttle to keep rpm in the proper range, and at the same time add right pedal pressure as needed to maintain heading.

Throughout the descent and until the time the skids are firmly on the ground and the collective is in the full down position, make necessary corrections with rudders to keep a constant heading. Make the necessary cyclic corrections to hold a level attitude and to prevent movements over the ground.

Errors

1. Cyclic overcontrolling during descent, resulting in movement over the ground on contact.

2. Failure to use collective smoothly.
3. Pulling back on the cyclic prior to or upon touchdown.
4. Failure to lower the collective smoothly and positively to the full down position upon ground contact.
5. Failure to maintain a constant rate of descent.
6. Failure to hold proper rpm.

Shallow Approach and Running Landing

A shallow approach and running landing are used when a high density altitude or a high gross weight condition or a combination thereof is such that a normal or steep approach can't be made because of insufficient power to hover. To compensate for this lack of power, a shallow approach and running landing makes maximum use of translational lift until ground contact is made. The glide angle is from 5-12 degrees, depending on wind conditions. Since a running landing follows the shallow approach, a ground area of sufficient length and smoothness must be available.

Start the shallow approach in the same manner as a normal approach except that a shallower angle of descent is maintained. The power reduction to begin the desired angle of descent will be less than that for a normal approach, since the angle of descent is less. As collective is lowered, maintain heading by increasing right rudder pressure, adjust throttle to maintain rpm, and use cyclic as necessary to hold the desired approach airspeed.

As in normal and steep approaches, the descent angle and rate of descent are primarily controlled by collective, and the ground speed is primarily controlled by the cyclic. The coordination of all controls is needed, however, if the approach is to be accomplished successfully.

Approach airspeed should be held until reaching an altitude of approximately 50-feet AGL. At this point, gradually apply aft cyclic to start losing airspeed. Coordinate a slight downward pressure on the collective to maintain the proper descent angle. Airspeed deceleration should be enough that the helicopter will settle to the ground, due to the decreased effect of translational lift just as the landing spot is reached.

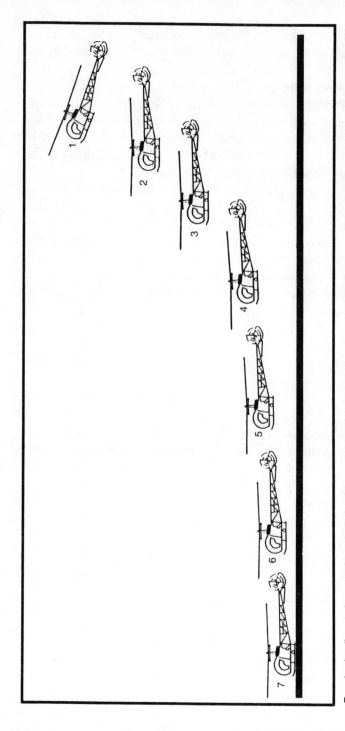

Running landing: 1. At approximately 50 ft AGL, raise nose slightly and slow airspeed for approach. 2-3. Bring the chopper to a level attitude and slow the rate of descent with the collective. 4-6. Use collective to continue slowing rate of descent and to cushion landing. 7. Continue skidding, braking with collective.

Deceleration must be smoothly coordinated, at the same time keeping enough lift to prevent the copter from settling abruptly.

On final approach, prior to making ground contact, place the helicopter in a level attitude with cyclic, use rudder to maintain heading, and cyclic necessary to keep heading and ground track identical. Allow the helicopter to settle gently to the ground in a straight and level attitude, cushioning the landing with the collective.

After ground contact, the cyclic is placed slightly forward of neutral to tilt the main rotor away from the tail boom; adjust throttle to hold rpm; maintain ground track with cyclic. Normally, the collective is held stationary after touchdown, until the helicopter comes to a complete stop. If braking action is desired or required, the collective may be lowered cautiously. To ensure directional control, normal rotor rpm must be maintained until the helicopter comes to a full stop.

Errors

1. Assuming excessive nose-high attitude at about 10 feet.
2. Insufficient collective and throttle to cushion the landing.
3. Failure to add left rudder as collective is added to cushion landing, resulting in a touchdown while in a left skid.
4. Touching down at an excessive ground speed.
5. Failure to touchdown in a level attitude.
6. Failure to maintain proper rotor rpm during and after touchdown.
7. Poor directional control upon touchdown.

10

AUTOROTATIONS

In helicopter flying, an autorotation is a maneuver that you can perform whenever the engine is no longer supplying power to the main rotor blades. A chopper transmission is designed to allow the main rotor hub and its blades to rotate freely in its original direction if the engine stops.

Keep in mind that at the instant of engine failure, the blades will be producing lift and thrust. By immediately lowering the collective, lift, as well as drag, will be reduced. This will cause the craft to begin an immediate descent, thus producing an upward flow of air through the rotor blades. The impact of this upward flow of air on the blades produces a ram effect which gives sufficient thrust to maintain rotor rpm throughout the descent. Since the tail rotor is driven by the main rotor during autorotation, heading control can still be maintained as if in normal flight.

Several factors affect the rate of descent in autorotation: density altitude, gross weight, rotor rpm and airspeed. Your primary control of the rate of descent is airspeed. Higher or lower airspeed is obtained with the cyclic, just as in normal flight.

You have a choice in angle of descent, varying from the vertical to maximum angle of descent or glide. Rate of descent is high at zero airspeed and decreases to a minimum somewhere in the neighborhood of 50-60 mph, depending on the particular copter and the factors just mentioned.

As the airspeed increases beyond that which gives you minimum rate of descent, the rate of your drop in altitude will again increase. When an autorotative landing is to be made, the energy stored in the rotating blades can be used to decrease the rate of descent even further and a safe landing made.

A greater amount of rotor energy is required to stop the helicopter with a high rate of descent than one that is descending more slowly. It follows, then, that autorotative descents at very low or very high airspeeds are more critical than those performed at the proper airspeed for the minimum rate of descent.

Each type of helicopter has a specific airspeed at which a power-off glide is most efficient. The best airspeed is the one which combines the greatest glide range with the slowest rate of descent. The specific airspeed is somewhat different for each type of copter, yet certain factors affect all configurations in the same manner. For specific autorotation airspeeds for a particular helicopter, refer to that particular helicopter's flight manual.

The exact airspeed for autorotation is established for each type of helicopter on the basis of average weather and wind conditions and normal loading. When operating a machine with excessive loads in high density altitudes or strong, gusty wind conditions, best performance is achieved from a slightly increased airspeed in the descent. On the other hand, for autorotations in light winds, low density altitudes and light loading, best performance is achieved from a slightly decreased normal airspeed. Following this general procedure of fitting airspeed to existing conditions, you can achieve approximately the same glide angle in any set of circumstances and estimate the probable touchdown point.

When making autorotative turns, generally use cyclic control only. Use of rudder pedals to assist or speed the turn only causes loss of airspeed and downward pitching of the craft's nose; especially when left pedal is used. When autorotation is initiated, sufficient right rudder should be used to

Nearly 800 Hughes TH-55A helicopter trainers were purchased by the U.S. Army during the late sixties.

maintain straight flight and to prevent yawing to the left. Don't change this rudder pressure to assist the turn.

If rotor rpm becomes too high during an autorotative approach, collective should be raised sufficiently to decrease rpm to the normal operating range, then lowered all the way again. This procedure may be repeated as necessary to keep rpm in the normal mode.

Due to the increased back cyclic pressure, which induces a greater airflow through the rotor system, rpm is most likely to increase above the maximum limit during the turn. The tighter the turn and the heavier the gross weight, the higher the rpm will be.

Hovering Autorotation

To practice hovering autorotations, establish the normal hovering altitude for your particular helicopter, considering its load and the atmospheric conditions, and keep it headed into the wind, holding maximum allowable rpm.

To enter autorotation, close the throttle quickly to ensure a clean split of the engine and rotor needles. This disengages the driving force of the engine from the rotor, thus eliminating torque effect. As throttle is closed, right rudder pressure must be applied to maintain heading. Usually, a slight amount of right cyclic will be necessary to keep the craft from drifting, but use cyclic control as required to ensure a vertical descent and a level attitude. Leave the collective pitch where it is on entry.

In helicopters with low inertia rotor systems, the aircraft will begin to settle immediately. Keep a level attitude, and ensure a vertical descent with the cyclic heading with the rudders, and apply up collective pitch as necessary to slow the descent and cushion the landing (generally, the full amount of collective is required). As upward collective is applied, the throttle will have to be held in the closed position to prevent the rotor from re-engaging.

Machines with high inertia rotor systems will maintain altitude momentarily after the throttle is closed. As rotor rpm decreases, the craft will start to settle. As it does so, apply upward collective, while holding the throttle in the closed position to slow the descent and cushion the landing. The

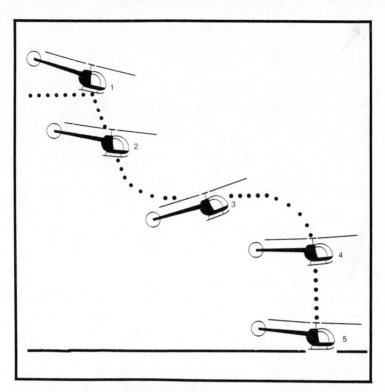

Autorotation: 1. Lower collective full-down, and close the throttle to "split the needles." 2. Maintain recommended autorotation speed. 3. Flare the craft to obtain the desired ground speed. 4-5. Move cyclic forward to level the helicopter, and increase collective to slow descent and cushion landing.

timing of this collective application, and the rate at which it is applied, depends on the particular helicopter being flown, its gross weight and the atmospheric conditions. Use cyclic to maintain a level attitude and to ensure a vertical descent. Keep heading with rudders.

When the weight of the helicopter is entirely on the skids, stop application of up collective. When the craft has come to a complete stop, lower the collective completely.

The timing of the collective is a most important consideration. If it's applied too soon, the remaining rpm will not be sufficient to effect a smooth landing. On the other hand, if collective is initiated too late, ground contact will be made before sufficient blade pitch is increased to cushion the landing.

Errors

1. Failure to use sufficient right rudder when power is reduced.
2. Failure to stop all sideward or fore and back movement with cyclic prior to touchdown.
3. Failure to time up collective properly, resulting in a hard touchdown.
4. Failure to touch down in a level attitude.

No-Flare Autorotation

The use of no-flare autorotations should be restricted to areas sufficiently long and smooth enough to permit a ground run. Know your helicopter and its limitations, as well as your own.

When the desired position for starting the autorotation has been reached, smoothly place the collective in the full down position, maintaining cruising rpm with the throttle. Decrease throttle quickly to ensure a clean split of the needles, and apply sufficient right pedal to maintain the desired heading. After splitting the needles, readjust the throttle so as to keep engine rpm well above normal idling speed but not high enough to cause the rejoining of the two needles. (Manufacturers will often recommend proper rpm for this use.)

Adjust attitude with cyclic to obtain the best gliding speed that will result in the slowest rate of descent. Be sure to hold collective in the full down position. If it's permitted to rise, rotor rpm will decrease due to the increased drag from the increased pitch angle of the blades. At about 50-feet AGL (check manufacturer's recommendation), raise the nose slightly to obtain the desired landing speed and to slow the rate of descent.

If a landing is to be made from the autorotative approach, rotate throttle to the closed or override position, and hold in this position as collective is raised, so the rotor will not re-engage. As the helicopter approaches normal hovering altitude, maintain a level attitude with the cyclic; heading with right rudder; apply sufficient collective (while holding the throttle in the closed position) to cushion touchdown; and be sure the craft is landing parallel to its direction of motion upon ground contact. Avoid landing on the heels of the skid gear. The timing of the collective application, and the amount applied, will be dependent on the rate of descent.

After ground contact is made, collective may be increased smoothly (still holding the throttle in the closed position), to keep the helicopter light on the skids and allow it to slow down gradually; or it may be held stationary, resulting in a shorter ground run; or it may be lowered cautiously for additional braking, if required, due to a fast touchdown and limited landing area. Hold cyclic slightly forward of neutral and use to keep directional control if landing is made in a crosswind. Maintain heading with rudders. In the event of insufficient rudder travel to maintain heading control when the rotor rpm decreases after touchdown, apply cyclic in the direction of the turn.

After the helicopter has stopped, decrease collective to the full down position. If a power recovery is to be made from the practice approach, replace certain of the above procedures with those found in "Power Recovery From Practice Autorotations," found in this chapter.

Errors

1. Failure to use sufficient right rudder when power is reduced.
2. Lowering the nose too abruptly when power is reduced, thus placing the craft in a dive.
3. Failure to maintain full down collective during the descent.
4. Application of up collective at an excessive altitude, resulting in a hard landing, loss of heading control and, possibly, damage to the tail rotor and main rotor blade stops.
5. Pulling the nose up just prior to touchdown.

Flare Autorotation

This maneuver enables you to land at any speed between a no landing run to that of a running one; that is to say, anywhere between a zero ground speed and the speed of touchdown from a no-flare autorotation. The speed at touchdown and the resulting ground run will depend on the rate and amount of the flare: The greater the degree of flare and the longer it is held, the slower the touchdown speed and the shorter the ground run. The slower the speed desired at touchdown from an autorotation, the more accurate must be the timing and speed of the flare, especially in craft with low inertia rotor systems.

Enter the flare autorotation in the same manner as the no-flare autorotation. The technique is the same down to the point where the flare is to begin. This point is slightly lower than the point at which the nose is raised in the no-flare autorotation.

At approximately 35-60-feet AGL, depending on the particular helicopter (check the manufacturer's recommendation), initiate the flare by moving the cyclic smoothly to the rear. Heading is maintained by the rudders. Care must be exercised in the execution of the flare so the cyclic isn't moved rearward so abruptly as to cause the helicopter to climb or so slowly as to allow it to settle so rapidly that the tail rotor strikes the ground.

As forward motion decreases to the desired ground speed, move the cyclic forward to a level attitude in preparation for landing. If a landing is to be made, rotate the throttle to the closed or override position. If power recovery is to be made, do so as the copter reaches the level position.

The altitude at this time should be about 3-10 feet, depending on the helicopter. If a landing is to be made, allow the craft to settle vertically. Apply collective smoothly as necessary to check the descent and cushion the landing. As collective pitch is increased, hold the throttle in the closed position so that the rotor will not re-engage. Additional right rudder is required to maintain heading, as collective is raised, due to the reduction in rotor rpm and the resulting reduced effect of the tail rotor.

After touchdown, when the chopper has come to a complete stop, lower the collective to the full down position.

Errors

1. Failure to use sufficient right rudder when power is reduced.

2. Lowering the nose too abruptly when power is reduced, thus placing the craft in a dive.
3. Failure to maintain full down collective during the descent.
4. Application of up collective at an excessive altitude, resulting in a hard landing, loss of heading control and possible damage to the tail rotor and the main rotor blade stops.
5. Applying up collective before a level attitude is attained: If timing is late, it may be necessary to apply up collective before a level attitude is attained.
6. Pulling the nose up just prior to touchdown on full autorotation.

Power Recovery From Practice Autorotations

A power recovery is used to terminate practice autorotations at a point prior to actual touchdown. If so desired, a landing can be made or a go-around initiated after the power recovery is made.

To effect a power recovery after the flare or level-off, coordinate upward collective and increase throttle to join the needles at operating rpm. The throttle and collective must be coordinated properly. If the throttle is increased too fast or too much, an engine overspeed will occur. If the throttle is increased too slow or too little in proportion to the increase in collective, a loss of rotor rpm will result. Use sufficient collective to check the descent, and coordinate left rudder with the increase in collective to maintain heading.

If a go-around is to be made, move the cyclic control smoothly forward to re-enter forward flight. If a landing is to be made following the power recovery, the helicopter can be brought to a hover at normal hovering altitude.

In transitioning from a practice autorotation to a go-around, care must be exercised to avoid an altitude-airspeed combination which could place the craft in an unsafe area of the height-velocity chart for that particular helicopter.

Errors

1. Initiating recovery too late, requiring a rapid application of controls, resulting in overcontrolling.

2. Failure to obtain and maintain a level attitude near the ground.
3. Adding throttle before the collective.
4. Failure to coordinate throttle and collective properly, resulting in an engine overspeed or loss of rpm.
5. Failure to coordinate left rudder with the increase in power.

11

PRACTICE MANEUVERS

The purpose of practice maneuvers is to build coordination and to keep you familiar with your aircraft and your own skill level. They give you the opportunity to practice many single maneuvers in one, by grouping them as a single unit. They also instill an automatic reflex to certain configurations.

Two major practice maneuvers are the S-turns and rapid deceleration or "quick-stop."

S-Turns

This single maneuver presents one of the most elementary problems in the practical application of a turn, and also for wind correction or drift while in a turn. To set up for S-turns, a reference line is used. This line can be a road, railroad, fence or section line, however, it should be straight for a considerable distance. It should extend as nearly perpendicular to the wind as possible.

The objective of the S-turn is to fly a pattern of two half-circle of equal size on opposite sides of a reference line. The maneuver should be started at an altitude of about 500-feet AGL and flown at a constant altitude above the terrain throughout. S-turns may be started at any point, however, during early training, it may be beneficial to start on a downwind heading.

As your helicopter crosses the reference line, a bank is immediately established. This initial bank will be the steepest used throughout the maneuver since the craft is headed directly downwind. The bank is gradually reduced as necessary to scribe a ground track in a half-circle. The turn should be timed so that as the rollout is completed, the helicopter is crossing the reference line, perpendicular to it and headed directly upwind.

A bank is immediately entered in the opposite direction to begin the second half of the S-turn. Since the copter is on an upwind heading, this, as well as the one just completed before crossing the reference line, will be the shallowest in the maneuver. The turn should gradually be increased as necessary to scribe a ground track which is a half-circle identical in size to the one previously completed on the other side of the reference line. The steepest bank in this turn should be attained just prior to rollout when the craft is approaching the reference line nearest to a downwind heading. This bank, along with the initial bank entered at the beginning of the maneuver, will be the steepest bank used in S-turns. The turn should be timed so that, as the rollout is completed, the helicopter is crossing the reference line perpendicular to it and headed directly downwind.

From here, the maneuver can be started over again without breaking the pattern. It can be continued as long as the reference line runs true without a break. You can do a number in one direction, then do a 180-degree turn and head back along the same track in the direction from which you just came.

As a summary, the angle of bank required at any given point in the maneuver is dependent on the groundspeed—the faster the groundspeed, the steeper the bank of the turn. Or, to express it another way, the more nearly the helicopter is to a downwind heading, the steeper the bank; the more nearly it is to an upwind heading, the shallower the bank.

In addition to varying the angle of bank to correct for wind drift in order to maintain the proper radius of turn, the chopper must also be flown with a drift correction angle (crab) in relation to its ground track, except, of course, when it's on direct upwind or downwind headings, or there's no wind. You

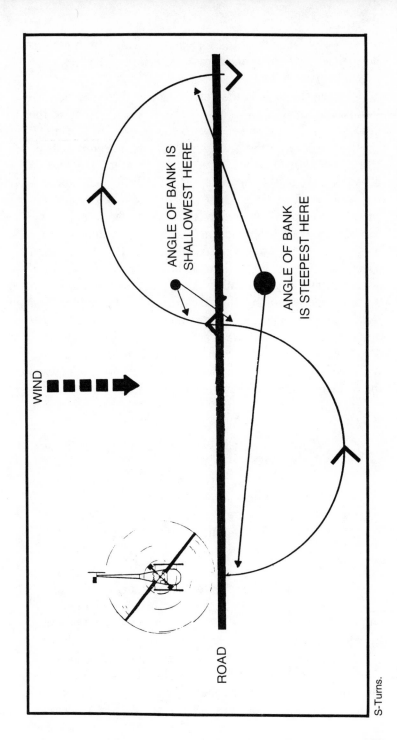

WIND

ANGLE OF BANK IS SHALLOWEST HERE

ANGLE OF BANK IS STEEPEST HERE

ROAD

S-Turns.

would normally think of the fore and aft axes of the craft as being tangent to the ground track pattern at each point, however, this isn't the case.

During the turn on the upwind side of the reference line (the side from which the wind is blowing), the nose of the helicopter will be crabbed toward the outside of the circle. During the turn on the downwind side of the reference line (the side opposite to the direction from which the wind is blowing), the nose of the helicopter will be crabbed toward the inside of the circle. In any case, the craft will be crabbed into the wind, just as if trying to maintain a straight ground track. The amount of crab depends on the wind speed and how close the ship is to its crosswind position. The higher the wind speed, the greater the crab angle at any given position for a scribed turn of a specific radius. The closer the helicopter is to a crosswind position, the greater the crab angle. The maximum crab angle should be at the point of each half-circle farthest from the reference line.

Standard radius for S-turns cannot be specified. This radius will depend on the airspeed of the helicopter, velocity of the wind and the initial bank angle required for the entry.

Errors

1. Failure to maintain two half-circles of equal distance from the reference line.
2. Too much or too little crab for crosswind.
3. Sloppy coordination on the controls.
4. Failure to cross reference line in level flight attitude.
5. Loss or gain in altitude during maneuver.

Quick Stops

Although used primarily for coordination practice, decelerations can be used to effect a quick stop in the air. The purpose of such a maneuver is to maintain a constant heading, altitude and rpm, while slowing the helicopter to a desired ground speed. It requires a high degree of coordination of all controls. It should be practiced at an altitude that will permit a safe clearance between tail rotor and the ground, especially at the point where the pitch attitude is highest. Telephone pole

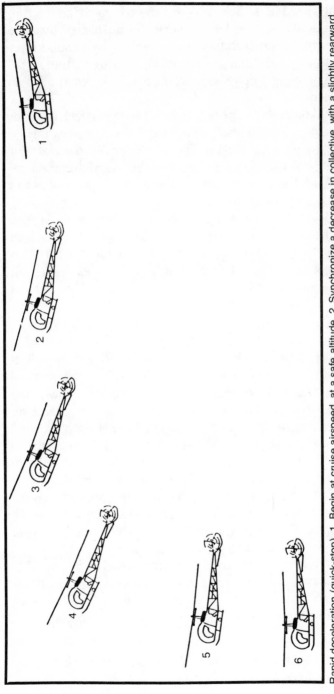

Rapid deceleration (quick-stop). 1. Begin at cruise airspeed, at a safe altitude. 2. Synchronize a decrease in collective, with a slightly rearward cyclic. 3–4. Continue with down collective and back cyclic to decrease groundspeed. 5. Bring cyclic forward and increase collective. 6. Follow through with a normal hover landing.

height should be sufficient, depending on type of craft flown. The altitude at completion should be no higher than the maximum, hovering altitude prescribed by the manufacturer. In selecting an altitude to begin the maneuver, the overall length of the helicopter and its height-velocity chart must be considered.

Although the maneuver is called a rapid deceleration or "quick stop," this doesn't mean that it should necessarily be used through to completion. The rate of deceleration is at your discretion, but blade "G" factors must be taken into consideration. A quick stop is completed when the helicopter comes to a hover during the recovery.

Begin the maneuver at a fast hover taxi speed, headed into the wind. An altitude should be selected that's high enough to avoid danger to the tail rotor during the flare, but low enough to stay out of the craft's shaded area throughout the maneuver, and also low enough that it can be brought to a hover during the recovery.

To start, decrease collective, simultaneously increasing rearward pressure on the cyclic. This rearward movement of the stick must be exactly timed to the lowering of the collective. If rearward cyclic stick is applied too fast, the craft will start to climb; if rearward cyclic is applied too slowly, the chopper will descend. The faster the decrease in collective, the more rapid should be the increase in rearward stick pressure, and the faster will be the deceleration. As collective is lowered, right rudder should be increased to maintain heading, and the throttle should be adjusted to maintain rpm.

Once speed has been reduced to the desired amount, recovery is initiated by lowering the nose and allowing the helicopter to settle to a normal hovering altitude, in level flight and zero ground speed or that desired.

During recovery, collective pitch should be increased as necessary to stop the craft at normal hovering altitude; throttle should be adjusted to maintain rpm; and left pedal pressure should be increased as necessary to maintain heading.

Errors

1. Failure to lead slightly with down collective on the entry.

2. Failure to raise the nose high enough, resulting in slow deceleration.
3. Applying back cyclic too rapidly initially, causing the helicopter to "balloon," gaining altitude suddenly.
4. Failure to lead with, and maintain, forward cyclic during recovery. If a quick stop isn't performed properly, it may be necessary to lead with collective, to prevent touching down too hard or on the heels of the skids.
5. Allowing the helicopter to stop forward motion in a tail low attitude.
6. Failure to maintain proper rpm.

Tree Topper

This maneuver is another coordination stratagem, one to practice using all controls in making minute corrections, while enjoing yourself. It's much like the S-turn, in that wind correction is involved.

Pick a wide-open area with a tree, pole or some object in the middle. Make sure there's good all around clearance. The objective is to look the chosen object over by moving your craft around it, as well as up and down.

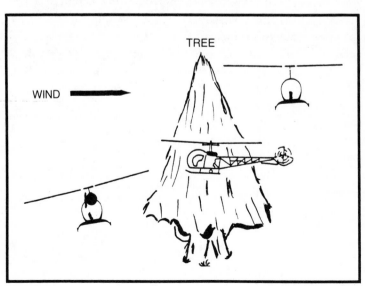

Tree Topper.

To start the maneuver, approach the object slowly from upwind at about hovering altitude. An upwind entry is desired to get the feel of wind speed and what it takes to stop short of the object.

Move to the object, being extremely careful not to touch it with blade tips. Notice your blade clearance. Move the helicopter lower and lower, gradually, making corrections with collective, cyclic, rudder and throttle. You should be moving forward, around the object, at the same time.

Once this has been done, move higher and higher, looking the object over. Again, extreme care should be used in keeping the blades away from the object. Make necessary corrections on the controls to keep the craft moving at a steady pace, keeping your distance from the object.

Once you've made a trip or two around it, and you have the feel of both the machine and wind, coordinating the controls, find another object and try the whole sequence over. Remember, caution is the word.

Errors

1. Failure to take into account the effect of wind as you move around the object.
2. Failure to coordinate controls with changes in collective, rpm and rudder, as you move up and down and around the object.
3. Failure to keep an equal distance from the object, as the craft moves around it. An equal-radius circle should be scribed on the ground.

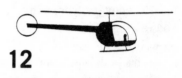

12

EMERGENCY PROCEDURES

Since emergency procedures differ with particular aircraft, before simulating any emergency, check the manufacturer's recommendations. There are, however, general emergency steps that every helicopter pilot should be familiar with, no matter what type of copter is being flown. It's the purpose of this chapter to acquaint you with this information.

Recovery From Low Rotor RPM

Recovery from low rotor rpm procedure is one used to return the rotor to normal operating rpm. This recovery is often referred to as "milking." If performed properly, it will normally regain lost rotor rpm while still maintaining flight. This condition is the result of having a high angle of attack on the main rotor blades, induced by too much collective. It creates a drag so great that engine power available, or being used, isn't sufficient to maintain normal rotor operating rpm.

When you realize what's happening, immediately add full throttle, and briskly decrease the collective to relieve, momentarily at least, the excess engine load. As the helicopter begins to settle, smoothly increase the collective, but only enough to stop the settling motion. Remember, down briskly, up smoothly and slower. This procedure, under critical conditions, might have to be repeated several times in order to regain normal rotor operating rpm. The amount that the collective can be decreased will depend on the altitude available at the time of the emergency condition. In practice, give yourself plenty of room to spare.

When operating at sufficient altitudes above the terrain, it will be necessary to decrease the collective only once to regain sufficient rotor rpm. When the rotor rpm begins to rise and attains about normal rotor operating rpm, anticipate decreasing the throttle slowly to prevent the engine from overspeeding.

If recovery from a low rotor rpm condition isn't effected soon enough, lifting power of the main rotor blades will be lost, as will rudder control.

This pedal control loss occurs as a result of the decrease in tail rotor rpm. Remember, the tail rotor is driven by the main rotor, and its rpm is directly proportional to that of the main rotor. If rudder control is lost and the altitude is such that a landing can be effected before the turning rate increases dangerously, decrease collective pitch slowly, maintain a level attitude with the cyclic and land.

Recovery From Blade Stall

Blade stall occurs when, at a high forward speed, the angle of attack of the retreating blade is made so acute that the streamline flow of air over its upper surface, especially toward blade tip, reaches the burbling point and begins breaking down. Each blade will stall when it becomes the retreating blade. The high angle of attack can also be increased beyond the "critical angle" and cause complete blade stall, as in such maneuvers as a steep turn or sudden up-gusts of air. Again, the airspeed at which blade stall commences will be reduced when the craft has a high, all-up weight or when it's at high altitudes, as a greater degree of collective must be used in these conditions.

You will first feel blade stall as a vibration equivalent to the number of blades in the main rotor, per revolution. That is to say, a three bladed rotor will have three vibrations per revolution, two bladers will have two, and so forth. The vibration can be fairly severe and a kicking at the controls can be present.

144

Aerospatiale 350C A Star.

When blade stall occurs, you can correct the situation by reducing the severity of the maneuver, reduce collective pitch, reduce airspeed/and increase rotor rpm, or combination thereof. It depends on your situation at the time.

A blade stall which is encountered because of the severity of a maneuver will normally correct itself, as soon as you reduce the harshness of, or cease entirely, the maneuver. This is applicable if the blade stall occurs in a steep turn, a sharp pull out at a high speed, etc.

In the majority of blade stall cases, reducing collective pitch is the right action, especially when flying fast in turbulent weather. In copters that are prone to high speed stalling of advancing blades (usually due to their reaching a high, critical, mach number), it's possible not to know which of the two possible causes is producing the vibrations felt. A slight reduction in rpm would, therefore, be advisable at the same time as the collective is lowered.

There's some debate against an immediate reduction of airspeed in the case of a blade stall at high cruising speed. Some feel the result of easing back on the cyclic would be to increase the G load and further aggravate stall symptoms. It's recommended that a reduction of airspeed should be accomplished slowly, and the collective should be lowered at the same time.

If higher rotor rpm can be used with a lower collective setting, then blade stall will occur at a higher cruising speed. In some helicopters, the possibility of reaching critical mach numbers with the advancing blades must be kept in mind when rpm is increased.

Much depends upon the type of helicopter being used as to the manner in which blade stall is induced. With some craft, blade-stall onset could be experienced frequently during routine exercises, however, in others extreme steep turns, with high G effects at altitude, may have to be carried out before blade stall is encountered.

Vortex Ring Condition

This situation can occur during a vertical descent through the air with power on, with a rate of descent in excess of 300 fpm usually being necessary. Although less common, it can also occur in conditions where considerable power is applied, with the helicopter mushing through the disturbed air. The latter case is generally only momentary but can cause considerable buffeting and a loss of lift.

In the case of the vertical descent, the effect can be prolonged, resulting in a high rate of descent, vibration and partial loss of control. The symptoms may vary among different helicopter types.

The vortex ring isn't dangerous, unless carried out at a low altitude. The rate of descent is high, both during the condition and recovery. Altitude should, therefore, not be held deliberately below 600-feet AGL. Steep or vertical approaches to small sites in calm air should be carried out at a low rate of descent in order to avoid the vortex ring condition.

This problem is so named because of the airflow pattern around the rotor. From the pilot's point of view, it may be thought of more simply as the fact that the rotor is forcing air downward, and the aircraft is then sinking into this downward-moving, disturbed air. It's not always easy to initiate the condition for demonstration purposes, as sideways, forward or backward movement through the air could prevent its occurring.

When the condition is encountered in a vertical descent, there are two main ways of recovery:

1. Easing the stick forward and diving out.
2. Entering autorotation; placing the collective full down and diving out.

Engine Failure

This emergency can happen any time, any place. It should be kept foremost in mind and a precautionary landing made any time there's indication of engine trouble. It's better to land with some power than none at all. Obviously, the most critical time for an engine out would be when working close to the ground in such attitudes as takeoff, landing or a low hover.

If time and altitude permit when engine failure occurs, rapidly reduce the main rotor's pitch with the collective a proportional amount to your altitude AGL. At an altitude of

300 feet and up, say, reduce collective to the maximum, which will reduce the rotor blade's pitch to a minimum. At altitudes of 10 feet or less, reduce the collective only a slight amount, if at all.

If altitude permits, obtain some forward airspeed. Transition to a forward glide advantageously reduces the rate of descent. From here, a normal landing without power can be made.

At an altitude of five to 10-feet AGL, rapidly increase the main rotor's pitch angle with the collective, depending on your rate of descent. You should make every effort to utilize all available rotor energy to cushion the landing. However, you should save some collective for the last few feet before touchdown.

If you're above 50-feet AGL, instantly execute an autorotative glide by applying appropriate forward cyclic and maximum down collective. This will permit the copter to descend along a forward path at complementary forward speed.

When approaching normal hovering altitude, apply backward cyclic to flare. This will reduce forward speed and further decrease the rate of descent. At about head high, five to eight-feet AGL, level the flare enough to bring the helicopter to an almost level attitude. A final cushioning effect with increased rotor blade pitch by up collective at approximately two to four feet AGL. This should set the craft nicely on the chosen spot.

After touchdown, turn battery switch, selector valve and ignition switch to the "off" position. Also place the mixture control in the "cut-off" position. Climb out of the craft, and you're home free.

Tail Rotor Control System Failure
Failure of the tail rotor is one of the more dangerous of helicopter emergencies, but if you're ready for it, for immediate action, it's just another emergency maneuver. Since it controls the directional stability of the craft, without the tail rotor, there's a tendency of the helicopter to begin turning in the opposite direction of the rotor blades, causing a landing or inflight problem, if forward speed gets too low.

Immediately go into an autorotative attitude and, maintain an airspeed sufficient to keep the craft aligned parallel with its forward ground track. Make an autorotational landing, while heading in a direction that's parallel to the flight or glide path. A "running landing" here would be most appropriate; enough so to keep the tail from swinging around.

Antitorque system failure could be the result of a failure in the tail rotor blades, the mechanical linkage between the rudders and the pitch-change mechanism of the tail rotor or the tail rotor drive-shaft between the transmission and the tail rotor.

If the system fails in cruising flight, the nose of the helicopter will usually pitch slightly and yaw to the right. The direction in which the nose pitches will depend on your particular craft and how it's loaded. Violence in pitching and yawing is generally greater when the failure occurs in the tail rotor blades and also is usually accompanied by severe vibration.

Pitching and yawing can be overcome by holding the cyclic stick near neutral and immediately entering autorotation. Keep cyclic movements to a minimum until the pitching subsides. Abrupt rearward movements of the cyclic should be avoided. If the stick is moved rearward too fast the main rotor blades could flex downward with sufficient force to strike the tail boom.

The fuselage will remain fairly well streamlined if sufficient forward speed is maintained. However, if you attempt a descent at slow speeds, a continuous turning movement to the left can be expected. Know the manufacturer's recommended speeds and procedures for each particular helicopter you fly. This will generally be found under "Emergency Procedures" in the aircraft flight manual. Directional control should be maintained primarily with cyclic and secondarily by gently applying throttle momentarily, with needles joined, to swing the nose to the right.

A running landing may be made or a flare-type. The best, and safest, landing technique, terrain permitting, is to land directly into the wind with about 20 mph airspeed. In a flare landing, the helicopter will turn to the left during the actual flare and subsequent vertical descent. An important factor to remember is that the craft should be level, or approximately level, at ground contact, in any case.

Immediate and quick action must be taken. The turning motion to the right builds up rapidly, because of the torque reaction produced by the relatively high power setting. To eliminate this turning effect, you should close the throttle immediately without varying collective pitch. Simultaneously, adjust the cyclic to stop all sideward or rearward movements and to level the chopper for touchdown. From this point, the procedure for a hovering autorotation is followed.

Low-Frequency Vibrations

Abnormal, low-frequency vibrations are always associated with the main rotor. These vibrations will be at some frequency related to the rotor rpm and the number of blades of the rotor, such as one vibration per rotor revolution, two per rev., three per rev., etc. Low frequency vibrations are slow enough that they can be counted.

The frequency and strength of the vibrations will cause you and/or your passengers to be noticeably bounced or shaken. If the vibration is felt through the cyclic, it'll have some definite kick at the same point in the rotor-blade cycle. These low-frequency vibrations can be felt in the fuselage, in the stick, or they can be evident in all simultaneously. Whether the tremor is in the fuselage or the stick will, to some extent, determine the cause.

Vibrations felt through the fuselage can be classified in four ways: lateral, longitudinal, vertical or a combination of the others. A lateral vibration is one which throws the pilot from side-to-side. A longitudinal vibration is one which rocks the pilot forward-and-backward, or in which the pilot receives a periodic kick in the back. A vertical vibration is one in which the pilot is bounced up-and-down, or it may be thought of as one in which the pilot receives a periodic "kick in the seat of the pants." Describing the vibrations to a mechanic in the above forms will also help him in determining the exact cause.

Vibrations felt through both the stick and fuselage are generally indicative of problems in the rotor or rotor support. A failure of the pylon support at the fuselage connection is also a possible cause.

If the low-frequency vibration in the fuselage occurs during translational flight or during a climb at certain airspeeds, the vibration could be a result of the blades striking their rest stops. This problem can be eliminated until mechanical correction by avoiding the flight conditions that cause it.

For low-frequency vibrations felt predominantly through the stick, the trouble is most likely in the control system linkage, from the stick to the rotor head.

Medium-Frequency Vibrations

In most helicopters, medium-frequency vibrations are a result of trouble with the tail rotor. Improper rigging, unbalance, defective blades or bad bearings in the tail rotor are all sources of this type vibrations. If it occurs only during turns, the trouble could be caused by insufficient tail-rotor flapping action. Medium-frequency vibrations are very difficult, if not impossible, to count, due to their fast rate. See a mechanic for a thorough check out.

High-Frequency Vibrations

These vibrations are associated with the engine in most helicopters and will be impossible to count, due to their high rate. However, they could be associated with the tail rotor in helicopters with tail rotor rpm about equal to, or greater than engine rpm. A defective clutch or missing or bent fan blade will cause vibrations. Any bad bearing in the engine, transmission or tail rotor drive shaft will result in vibrations with frequencies directly related to the speed of the engine.

Experience in detecting and isolating the three main different classes of vibrations when they first develop makes it possible to correct the situation long before it becomes serious. Take a good look, feel and listen. If you don't like what you find, see a mechanic.

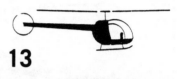

13

SPECIAL OPERATIONS

A special operation is one that is out of the ordinary. Such an operation would include flight in confined areas, high, low and ground reconnaissance maneuvers.

Slope Operations

Approaching a slope, mountain, hill or knoll for landing isn't much different from an approach to any other helicopter landing area. However, during this type of operation, an allowance must be made for wind, obstacles, and a possible forced landing. Since the terrain incline could constitute a barrier to the wind, turbulence and down-drafts must be anticipated because of air spilling over and down.

It's usually best to land the helicopter cross-slope rather than upslope. And, landing downslope or downhill is definitely *not* recommended because of the possibility of striking the tail rotor on the ground during normal flare out.

Manuever slowly toward the incline, being especially careful not to turn the tail upslope. The helicopter should be hovered in a position cross-slope, directly over the spot of intended landing.

A slight downward pressure on the collective will put the copter in a slow descent. As the upslope skid touches the ground, apply cyclic pressure in the direction of the slope.

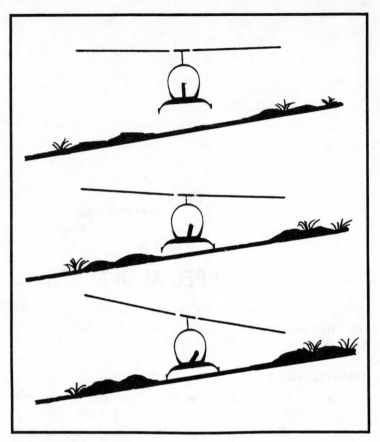

Slope landing and takeoff.

This will hold the skid against the incline, while you continue a gradual letdown with the collective.

As collective is reduced, continue to move the cyclic toward the slope as needed to maintain a fixed position. The slope must be shallow enough to allow you to hold the craft against it with the cyclic during the entire landing.

A five-degree slope is considered maximum for normal operation of most helicopters. Each make of machine will generally let you know in its own particular way when you're about to run out of lateral cyclic, such as the rotor hub hitting the rotor mast, vibrations felt through the cyclic, etc. If you encounter such warnings, don't land. They indicate the slope is too steep for safe operations.

Aerospatiale SA 365.

Once the downslope skid has touched the ground, continue to lower the collective until reaching the stop. Maintain normal rotor operating rpm until the full weight of the chopper rests on the skids. This will assure adequate rotor rpm for immediate takeoff if the craft should start to slide downhill. Use the rudders as necessary throughout the landing to maintain heading.

The procedure for a slope takeoff is almost the exact reverse of that for a slope landing. Adjust the throttle to obtain takeoff rotor rpm and slowly move the cyclic in the direction of the slope so that the rotor rotation plane is parallel to the true horizontal rather than the slope. Apply up-collective smoothly. As the helicopter becomes light on the skids, apply rudders as needed to maintain heading.

Upon raising the downslope skid and the helicopter approaches a level attitude, return the cyclic to the neutral position. Continue to apply up collective, taking the craft straight up to a hover, before moving away from the slope. As you depart, care should be taken that the tail doesn't turn upslope. Remember the danger of the tail rotor striking the ground.

Errors

1. Failure to maintain proper rotor rpm throughout the entire maneuver.
2. Letting the craft down too rapidly.
3. Failure to adjust cyclic to keep the craft from sliding downhill.

Confined Area Operations

A confined area is a local where the flight of your helicopter is limited in some direction by terrain or the presence of obstructions, natural or man made: a clearing in the woods, a city street, a road, a building roof, etc.

Barriers on the ground, or the ground itself, can interfere with the smooth flow of air, resulting in turbulence. This interference is transmitted to upper air levels as larger, but less, intense disturbances. Therefore the greatest turbulence is usually found at low altitudes. Gusts are unpredictable variations in wind velocity. Ordinary gusts are dangerous only in slow flight at very low altitudes. You might be unaware of such a gust. Its cessation could reduce airspeed below that required to sustain flight, due to the loss of effective translational lift. Gusts cannot be planned for or anticipated. Turbulence, however, can generally be predicted. You'll find turbulence in the following areas, when wind velocity exceeds 10 mph:

1. Near the ground on the downwind side of trees, buildings, hills or other obstructions. The turbulence area is always relative in size to that of the obstacle, and relative in intensity to the speed of the wind.
2. Near the ground on the immediate upwind side of any solid obstacle, such as trees in leaf and buildings. This condition isn't generally dangerous, unless the wind velocity is 15 knots or higher.
3. In the air, above and slightly downwind of any sizable obstruction, such as a hill or mountain range. The size of the obstruction and the wind speed govern the height to which the turbulence extends and also its severity.

You should know the direction and approximate speed of the wind at all times. Plan landings and takeoffs with the wind conditions in mind. This doesn't necessarily mean that takeoffs and landings should always be made into the wind, but wind must be considered, and its velocity will, many times, determine proper avenues on approach and takeoff.

In case of engine failure, plan flights over areas suitable for forced landing, if possible. You might find it necessay to choose between a crosswind approach over an open area and one directly into the wind but over heavily wooded or extremely rough terrain where a safe forced landing would be impossible. Perhaps the initial approach phase can be made crosswind over the open area, and then it may be possible to execute a turn into the wind for the final approach portion.

Always operate the copter as closely to its normal capabilities as possible while considering the situation at hand. In all confined area operations, with the exception of the pinnacle operation, of course, the angle of descent should be no steeper than is necessary to clear any barrier in the avenue of approach and still land on the pre-selected spot. The angle of climb on takeoff shouldn't be any steeper than is necessary to clear any barrier. It's far better to clear the barrier by just a few feet and maintain normal rotor operating rpm with, perhaps, a reserve of power, than it is to clear the obstruction by a wide margin but with dangerously low rotor rpm and no power reserve.

Always make the landing to a specific point and not to just some general area. The more confined the area the more essential it is that you land the helicopter precisely on a definite point. Keep this spot in sight during the entire final approach phase.

Any increase in elevation between the point of takeoff and the point of intended landing must be given due consideration, because sufficient power must be available to bring the chopper to a hover at the point of the intended landing. A decrease in wind speed should also be allowed for with the presence of obstructions.

If you're flying a helicopter near obstructions, it's critical that you consider the tail rotor. Therefore, a safe angle of descent over barriers must be established to ensure tail rotor clearance. After coming to a hover, avoid swinging the tail into obstructions.

Make a high reconnaissance to determine the suitability of the area for a landing. In a high reconnaissance, the following items should be accomplished:

1. Determine wind direction and speed.
2. Select the most suitable flight paths in and out of the area, with particular consideration being given a forced landing.
3. Plan the approach and select a touchdown point.
4. Locate and determine the size of obstacles immediately around the chosen area.

A high reconnaissance is flown at about 500-feet AGL, however, a higher altitude may be required in some craft.

Always ensure sufficient altitude to land into the wind in case of engine failure. This means the greatest altitude will be

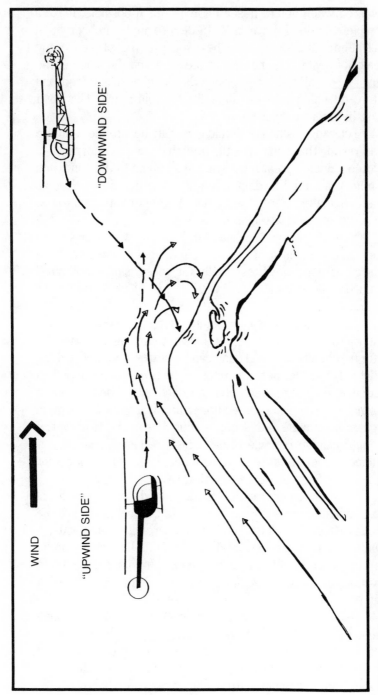

WIND

"UPWIND SIDE"

"DOWNWIND SIDE"

Windflow over mountain and its effect on aircraft.

required when you're headed downwind. If possible, make a complete circle of the area. A 45-degree angle of observation will generally allow you to best analyze the presence and height of obstacles, the size of the area and the slope of the terrain. Safe altitudes and airspeeds should be maintained, and a forced landing area should be kept within reach. This point can't be overemphasized.

Your approach path should generally be into the wind and over terrain that minimizes the time that you're out of reach of a forced-landing area. If by flying at an angle to the wind, you can keep a forced landing area in reach, then do so. If at all possible, make a normal approach. A steeper approach will be required, if there are high obstacles.

Now, in the low reconnaissance, verify what was seen in the high reconnaissance. Pick up anything that you could have missed earlier. Check especially for wires, slopes and small crevices, because these are particularly difficult to see from a higher altitude.

A low reconnaissance begins just after your approach entry into the confined area. It ends at touchdown. During the interim, objects on the ground can be better identified and the height of obstacles better estimated. The view of the approach path is greatly improved. The approach should be as close to normal as possible. If new information warrants a change in flight path or angle of descent, it should be made. However, if a major change in angle of descent is required, make a go-around. If a go-around decision is made, it should be done prior to losing effective translational lift.

Once the commitment is made to land, the approach will be terminated in a hover at an altitude that will conserve the ground effect. Check the landing spot carefully before actually landing. Maintain rotor operating rpm until the stability of the helicopter on the terrain can be checked for a secure and safe position. In many cases, not doing so could mean a long walk out.

Before taking off from a confined area, make a walking ground reconnaissance to determine the point from which it should be initiated. This is to ensure a maximum amount of available area, and how best to get the helicopter from the landing spot to a position from which the takeoff is proposed.

First thing, check the wind. If the rotor was left turning after landing, walk a sufficient distance from the craft to ensure that the downwash of the blades doesn't interfere. Light dust or grass may be dropped and the direction they are blown observed.

Next, go to the downwind end of the area, and mark a position for takeoff, so that the tail and main rotors will have sufficient clearance from obstructions. A sturdy marker, such as a heavy stone or log, should be used as this marker.

If rearward flight is required to reach the takeoff position, reference markers should be placed in front of the helicopter in such a way that a ground track can be safely followed to the takeoff position. If wind conditions and available area permit, hover-taxi downwind from the landing position to the takeoff spot.

In preparing for the actual takeoff from a confined area, first visualize the angle over obstacles from the takeoff position. The flight path should be over the lowest barrier that allows for taking best advantage of wind and terrain. Make the takeoff and climb as near normal as possible. Again, it's better to clear the obstructions by a few feet at normal rotor rpm than to sacrifice rotor rpm by attempting to clear by a large margin. Wind conditions should seriously be considered during the takeoff.

In general, flying over good terrain is preferable to heading directly into the wind, depending, of course, on the speed of the wind and the relative height of obstacles.

Because of its unique flight characteristics, a helicopter is capable of many missions no other aircraft can perform. You must, however, realize the hazards involved and know also what precautions to take in preserving the craft, as well as your life.

Here are a few basic and general precautionary rules that you should consider and keep in mind:

1. Don't perform acrobatic maneuvers.
2. Don't check magnetos in flight in lieu of ground checks during runup.
3. Use caution when adjusting mixture in flight.
4. Always taxi (air) slowly (about as fast as you can walk).

5. Always check balance prior to flying.

6. Use caution when hovering on the leeward side of buildings or obstruction.

7. Don't hover at an altitude that will place you in the shaded area of the height-velocity chart.

8. Always hover for a moment before beginning a new flight.

9. When practicing hovering turns, sideward flight and similar low airspeed maneuvers, be especially careful to maintain proper rpm.

10. When flying in rough, gusty air, use special care to maintain proper rpm.

11. Always clear the area overhead, ahead, to each side and below before entering practice autorotations.

12. Make sure any object placed in the cockpit of your helicopter is secured to prevent fouling of controls or mechanisms.

13. Except in sideward or rearward flight, always fly the aircraft from references ahead.

Rotor RPM Operating Limits

Limits of rotor rpm vary with each type of craft. In general, the lower limit is determined primarily by the control characteristics of a particular helicopter during autorotation. Since the tail rotor is driven by the main rotor, a minimum main rotor rpm exists at which tail rotor thrust is sufficient for proper heading control. Below this minimum main-rotor rpm, full rudder travel will not maintain heading under certain conditions of flight.

The upper limit for rotor rpm is based on both autorotative characteristics and structural strength of the rotor system. Structural tests, plus an adequate margin for safety, are required by FAA safety standards for the certification of the aircraft.

Extreme Attitudes and Overcontrolling

Avoid all maneuvers which would place the craft in danger of extreme and unusual attitudes. Design characteristics of a helicopter preclude the possibility of safe inverted flight.

Avoid helicopter loading that will cause an extreme tail-low attitude when taking off to a hover. Aft center CG is dangerous while hovering, and even more so in flight because of limited forward cyclic travel.

Avoid heavy loading forward of the CG. The result is limited aft cyclic travel, endangering controllability.

Avoid an extreme nose-low attitude when executing a normal takeoff. Such an attitude may require more power than the engine can deliver, and it will also allow the helicopter to settle to the ground in an unsafe landing attitude. In the event of a forced landing, only a comparatively level attitude can assure a safe touchdown.

Avoid abrupt applications of rearward cyclic. The violent backward-pitching action of the rotor disc may cause the main rotor to flex downward into the tailboom.

Avoid large or unecessary movements of the cyclic, while in a hover. Such movements of the cyclic can, under certain conditions, cause sufficient loss of lift to make the craft settle to the ground.

Flight Technique in Hot Weather

As discussed in an earlier chapter, hot temperatures drive density altitude up. When you encounter hot weather, piloting skill calls for special techniques. Follow these rules religiously:

1. Make full use of wind and translational lift.
2. Hover as low as possible and no longer than absolutely necessary.
3. Maintain maximum allowable engine rpm.
4. Accelerate very slowly into forward flight.
5. Employ running takeoffs and landings, whenever possible.
6. Use caution in maximum performance takeoffs and landings from steep approaches.
7. Avoid high rates of descent in all approaches.

High Altitude Pilot Technique

Of the three major factors limiting helicopter performance at high altitudes (gross weight, density altitude and wind), only gross weight may be controlled by the pilot of an unsupercharged helicopter. At the expense of range, you may carry smaller amounts of fuel to improve performance, increase the number of passengers or the amount of baggage. Where practical, use running landings and takeoffs. Make maximum use of favorable winds, with landings and takeoffs directly into them when possible. Other factors sometimes dictate otherwise.

When the wind blows over large obstructions, such as mountain ridges, turbulent conditions are set up. The wind blowing up the slope on the windward side is usually relatively smooth. However, on the leeward side, the wind spills rapidly down the slope, similar to the way water flows down a rough streambed. This tumbling action sets up strong downdrafts and causes very turbulent air. These violent downdrafts can cause aircraft to strike the sides of mountains. Therefore, when approaching mountain ridges against the wind, make an extra altitude allowance to assure safe terrain clearance. Where pronounced mountain ridges and strong winds are present, a clearance of 2000- 3000-feet AGL is considered a desirable minimum. Also, it's advisable to climb to the crossing altitude well before reaching the mountain barrier to avoid having to make the climb in a persistent downdraft.

When operating over mountainous terrain, fly on the upwind side of ridges. The safest approach is usually made lengthwise of the ridge at about a 45-degree angle. Fly near the upwind edge to avoid possible downdrafts and to be in position to autorotate down the upwind side of the slope in case of forced landing. Riding the updraft in this manner results in a lower rate of descent, improved glide ratio, and a greater choice of a landing areas.

Tall Grass and Water Operations

Tall grass will tend to disperse or absorb the ground cushion that you're used to over firm ground. More power will be required to hover, and takeoff could be tricky. Before attempting to hover over tall grass, make sure that at least two to three inches more manifold pressure are available than is required to hover over normal terrain.

Operations over water with a smooth or glassy surface makes altitude determination difficult. Exercise caution to prevent the helicopter from inadvertently striking the water. This problem doesn't exist over rough water, but a very rough water surface could disperse the ground effect and thereby require more power to hover. Movements of the water surface, wind ripples, waves, current flow or even agitation by the chopper's own rotor wash, will tend to give you a false sense of aircraft movement.

Carburetor Icing

Carburetor icing is a frequent cause of engine failure. The vaporization of fuel, combined with the expansion of air as it passes through the carburetor, causes a sudden cooling of the mixture. The temperature of the air passing through the carburetor can drop as much as 60-degrees F within a fraction of a second. Water vapor in the air is squeezed out by this cooling, and if the temperature in the carburetor reaches 32-degrees F or below, the moisture will be deposited as frost or ice inside the carburetor passages. Even a slight accumulation of such deposits reduces power and can lead to a complete engine failure, particularly when the throttle is partially or fully closed.

On dry days or when the temp is well below freezing, moisture in the air isn't generally enough to cause much trouble. But, if the temperature is 20-70-degrees F, with visible moisture or high humidity, the pilot should be constantly on the alert for carb ice. During low or closed throttle settings, an engine is particularly susceptible to carburetor icing.

Indications of carb ice include unexplained loss of rpm or manifold pressure; the carburetor air temp indicating in the "red" (danger) arc or "yellow" (caution) arc; and engine roughness. A loss of manifold pressure will generally give the first indication. However, due to the many small control changes (settings) made in the throttle and collective, this might be less noticeable. So, a close check of the carb air temperature gauge is necessary so that carburetor heat may be adjusted to keep the carb air temp gauge out of the red and yellow arcs.

Carburetor air temperature gauges are marked with a green arc, representing the range of desired operating temps; a yellow arc represents the range of temperatures in which caution should be exercised, since icing is possible; and a red arc represents the maximum operating temperature limit, or is used to represent the most dangerous range in which carb ice can be anticipated. The carb heat control should be adjusted so that the carburetor air temperature remains in the green arc.

The carburetor heater is an anti-icing device that preheats air before it reaches the carburetor. This preheating can be used to melt ice or snow entering the intake duct; melt ice that forms in the carburetor passages (provided the accumulation isn't too great); and to keep the fuel mixture above the freezing point, preventing formation of carb ice.

When conditions are favorable for carb ice, you should make the proper check for its presence often. Check the manifold pressure gauge reading, then apply full carburetor heat and leave it on until you're certain that if ice was present, it has been removed. (During this check, a constant throttle and collective setting should be maintained.) Carb heat should then be returned to the "off" position (cold). If the manifold pressure gauge indicates higher than when the check was started, and carb air temp gauges indicates a safe operation range, carb ice has been removed.

Fuel injection systems have replaced carburetors in some craft. In the fuel injection system, the fuel is normally injected into the system either directly ahead of the intake valves or into the cylinders themselves. In the carburetor system, the fuel enters the airstream at the throttle valve. The fuel injection system is generally considered to be less susceptible to icing than the carb system.

Effect of Altitude on Instrument Readings

The thinner air of higher altitudes causes the airspeed indicator to read slow in relation to True Airspeed. True airspeed may be roughly computed by adding to the Indicated Airspeed two per cent of the indicated airspeed for each 1000 feet of altitude MSL. For example, an indicated speed of 80 mph at 5000-feet MSL will be a True airspeed of about 88 mph. This computation may be made more accurately with the use of a computer.

Manifold pressure is reduced approximately one inch per 1000 feet above sea level. If you have 28-inches manifold pressure at 1000 feet, only 22-inches manifold pressure will be available at 7000. This loss of manifold pressure must be considered when planning flights to higher altitudes.

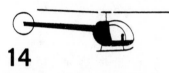

14
INTRODUCTION TO THE
HELICOPTER FLIGHT MANUAL

It's your responsibility as pilot in command (PIC) to know all pertinent information for each helicopter you fly. The helicopter flight manual is designed to provide you with a general knowledge of the particular helicopter and the information necessary for its safe and efficient operation. Its function isn't to teach you to fly but, rather, to provide you with the best possible operating instructions, under most circumstances. The manual isn't intended as a substitute for sound judgement, however, as emergencies and other unforeseen situations may require modification of these procedures.

A helicopter flight manual accompanies each certificated helicopter. Although the manual for a particular craft may contain information identical to that contained in the flight manual for other helicopters of the same make and model, it may also contain data which is peculiar only to that one helicopter, especially the information on weight and balance. Helicopter flight manuals are prepared and furnished by the aircraft's manufacturers. Much of the information contained in them is required by FARs, Part 27, "Airworthiness Standards: Normal Category Rotorcraft." However, manufacturers often include additional information that is helpful to the pilot but which isn't specifically required.

When the helicopter manual contains information required by regulations that doesn't appear as placards in the craft, the manual must be carried in the machine at all times. The statement, "This document must be carried in the aircraft at all times," will appear somewhere on the manual if such conditions exist.

Most flight manuals would include the following, under chapters, sections, headings or a similar breakdown in information:

General Information
Limitations
Normal Procedures
Emergency and Malfunction Procedures
Performance Data
Weight & Balance
Aircraft Handling, Servicing & Maintenance

General Information

Data presented here would include an introduction, if there is one, method of presentation, helicopter description, certification, design and construction, and general dimensional data.

The Introduction might read someting to the effect: "The pilot's flight manual has been prepared with but one very fundamental goal in mind; that is, to provide the pilot with all information necessary to accomplish the intended mission with the maximum amount of safety and economy possible..."

The method of presentation means just that: Information in various sections is presented in different formats. It can be presented as a narrative, charts, tabular form, etc., or a combination. In any case, it will be described here. Notes, step-by-step procedures are also explained, such as the following examples:

The "Caution" symbol is used to alert you that damage to equipment could result, if the procedure step isn't followed exactly.

The "Warning" symbol is used to bring to your attention that not only damage to equipment but personal injury could occur, if the instruction is disregarded.

The Helicopter Description gives an overall description of the craft. It may describe it as fast, lightweight, turbine-powered, all-purpose, etc. It would also give other key tidbits, such as its different uses and configurations: ambulance, internal/external cargo capability, aerial survey, patrol, photographic, air/sea rescue, agricultural, forestry and police applications, to name a few.

"Design and Construction" gives details as to material make-up, crew and passenger seating, power-plant and some of the craft's outstanding features, among others.

As an example, one entry in the Hughes 500D (Model 369D) explains: "...is a turbine powered, rotary-wing aircraft constructed primarily of aluminum alloy. The main rotor is

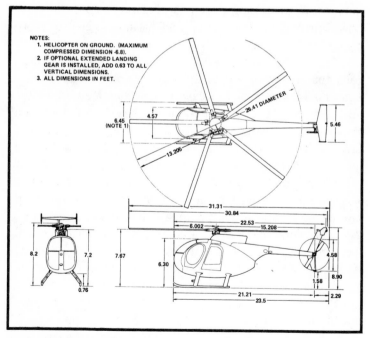

369D Helicopter principal dimensions.

five-bladed and fully articulated, the tail rotor is a two-bladed, antitorque semi-rigid type. Power from the turboshaft engine is coupled to the main and tail rotors by drive shafts and two transmissions. An overrunning (one-way) clutch in the drive between the engine and main transmission permits free-wheeling of the rotors for autorotational descent."

"General Dimensional Data" would include rotor characteristics, rotor speeds, control rigging of the main and tail rotor. Often general information graphs and charts are included for such conversions dealing with velocity, temperature, liquid, linear, weight and pressure. Also, a three-view drawing of the particular craft, showing its principal dimensions may be included.

Limitations

All aircraft have certain parameters within which they must fly. With the helicopter, these limitations would include airspeed limits, rotor-speed, weight and balance, powerplant and others. In some instances, limitations are as easy to comply with as keeping a needle within a green or yellow arc, while others, such as weight and balance, will take more thought and preplanning.

This section would include all important operating limitations that must be observed during normal operations. Airspeed Limits must be shown on the airspeed indicator (ASI) by a color coding or must be displayed in the form of a placard. A red radial line must be placed on the ASI to show the airspeed limit beyond which operation is dangerous. This speed is also known as the "never-exceed" speed or Vne. A yellow arc is used to indicate cautionary operating ranges, and of course, a green arc for safe or normal operation. Required information on Rotor Limits are marked on the tachometer by red radial lines and yellow arcs respectively, with normal operating ranges marked with a green arc, much as speed markings. Information for rotor limits, as well as airspeed, is sometimes given in the form of a chart or graph.

Powerplant limitation information will explain all powerplant limits and the required markings on the powerplant instruments. This will include such items as fuel octane rating, idling rpm, manifold pressure, oil pressure, oil temperature, cylinder-head temp, fuel pressure, mixture and others.

Normal Procedures

This section of the manual contains information concerning normal procedures for takeoff and landing, appropriate airspeeds peculiar to the rotorcraft's operating characteristics and other pertinent information necessary for safe operations. This portion may include the following procedures: checklists for preflight, before starting engine, starting engine, warmup, takeoff, inflight procedures and landing.

Normal procedures would also include such operations as low-speed maneuvering, practice autorotations, doors-off flight and post flight. Depending on the machine, of course, it could give you an instrument panel rundown, explain pilot controls and even give you a rundown on the fuel system.

Engine Start Procedures:

1. Mixture, IDLE CUT-OFF.
2. Fuel valve, ON.
3. Throttle friction released, Throttle closed.
4. Fuel boost, ON; check pressure.
5. Mixture FULL-RICH, 2.5-3.0 seconds; return to IDLE CUT-OFF.
6. Fuel boost, OFF.
7. Ignition switch, BOTH.
8. Engage starter.
9. When engine starts, mixture FULL-RICH.
10. Heater fan (exhaust muff heater), ON.
11. Set engine rpm at approximately 1400.
12. Fuel boost, ON.
13. Check engine oil pressure 25 psi minimum.
14. Alternator switch, ON.

Emergency & Malfunction Procedures

These procedures may warrent a section of their own, or they could be combined with "Normal Operating Procedures." However, in either case, they should be studied, until they

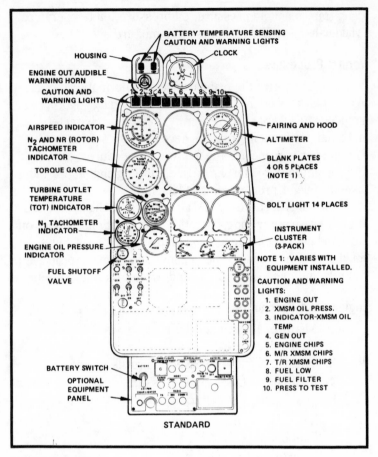

Instrument Panel

become second nature to you, and marked off for quick reference.

This section should cover such items as engine failure, ditching, tail rotor failure, and how to recognize and correct such emergencies. It would also contain failure of specialized, optional equipment, such as cyclic trim or the power turbine governor.

Recommendations for correcting such situations may read like this example on engine failure:

1. Establish a 60 mph autorotation.
2. If less than 2000-feet AGL, pick a landing spot, and proceed with autorotation landing.

3. Pull mixture control to IDLE CUT-OFF, when time permits, to stop flow of fuel from nozzles.
4. If altitude permits (cyclic can be gripped between knees to achieve the following):
   a. With mixture in IDLE CUT-OFF.
   b. Throttle—crack about ½ inch.
   c. Starter—press to engage.
   d. Mixture—push to FULL RICH position when engine fires.

   (Note: If fuel boost pump was on at time of engine stoppage, a flooded condition could have resulted, necessitating additonal use of the starter.)

Performance Data

It's primarily from the information taken from graphs and charts found in this section that you're able to plot and figure how the craft will operate. This section should include such information as: rates of climb and hovering ceilings, together with the corresponding airspeeds and other pertinent information, including the calculated effect of altitude and temperature, maximum allowable wind for safe operation near the ground, and sufficient other data to outline the limiting heights and corresponding speeds for safe landing after power failure.

Using the Density Altitude and Best Rate of Climb Speed charts, find the best rate of climb speed you should use when at a pressure altitude of 7000 feet with a temperature of 20 degrees C.

1. Locate 20 degrees C along the bottom of the DA chart. Follow its line vertically, until it intersects 7000-feet pressure altitude. Move horizontally left to read a density altitude of approximately 9000 feet.

2. Using the Best Rate Of Climb chart, locate 9000-feet DA on the left side. Move horizontally from this point until intersecting the dark vertical line. From this point drop vertically straight down the graph to the craft's best rate of climb speed of 59-60 knots.

"Maximum allowable wind" for safe operations near the ground will be noted by a statement in most flight manuals, similiar to the following: "When hovering with wind from the

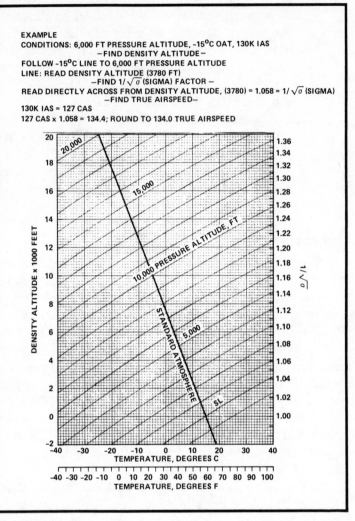

EXAMPLE
CONDITIONS: 6,000 FT PRESSURE ALTITUDE, -15°C OAT, 130K IAS
—FIND DENSITY ALTITUDE—
FOLLOW -15°C LINE TO 6,000 FT PRESSURE ALTITUDE
LINE: READ DENSITY ALTITUDE (3780 FT)
—FIND 1/√σ (SIGMA) FACTOR —
READ DIRECTLY ACROSS FROM DENSITY ALTITUDE, (3780) = 1.058 = 1/√σ (SIGMA)
—FIND TRUE AIRSPEED—
130K IAS = 127 CAS
127 CAS x 1.058 = 134.4; ROUND TO 134.0 TRUE AIRSPEED

Density Altitude Chart

left, expect random yaw oscillations; with wind from right, expect random pitch and roll oscillations in winds 10 knots and above."

Limiting heights and corresponding speeds for safe landing after power failure are generally incorporated in a chart called the "Airspeed vs. Altitude Limitations Chart" or "Height-Velocity Curve, Diagram or Chart." This chart generally appears in the performance section of the manual, but occasionally can be found in the "Operating Limitations Section."

You'll notice in the Height-Velocity Chart presented here the recommended takeoff profile. A normal takeoff would be to lift off to about eight feet AGL and accelerate to around 36 knots, before initiating a climb. Once the climb is started, it recommends a gradual increase in airspeed to 60 knots as a height of 75-feet AGL is attained.

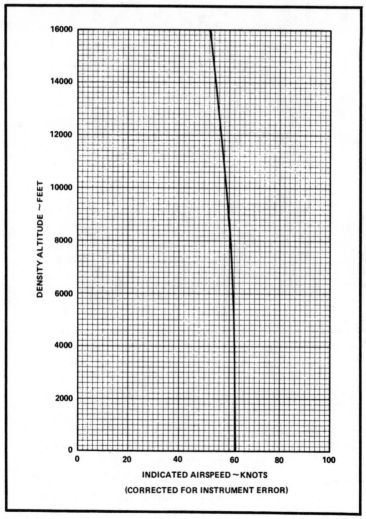

Speed for Best Rate of Climb.

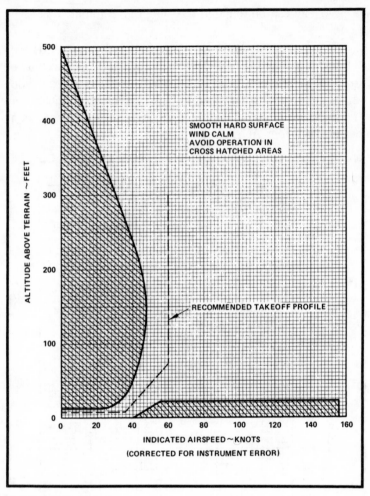

Height Velocity Diagram.

Care should be taken to avoid operations within the shaded area of the Height-Velocity Chart, as it signifies an unsafe operation.

All helicopters will normally have at least one placard displayed in a conspicuous position that has a direct and important bearing on safe operation of that particular helicopter. These placards will generally appear also in the machine's flight manual in the "Operating Limitations" section under the heading of "Placards, Caution or Warning." An example of this might be, "Strobe anticollision lights should be turned OFF during prolonged hover or ground operation over concrete, to avoid possible pilot distraction." Another example might be, "Solo pilot operation from the LEFT seat only."

Weight & Balance

The Weight & Balance portion must include rotorcraft weights and center-of-gravity (CG) limits, together with the items of equipment on which the empty weight is based. This will generally require the use of a chart or graph from which you can compute the CG position for any given loading situation.

If the unusable fuel supply in any tank exceeds one gallon or five percent of the tank capacity, whichever is greater, a warning shall be provided to indicate to flight personnel that when the quantity indicator reads "zero" the remaining fuel in the tank can't be used for flight. A complete explanation and sample problem on weight and balance follows in the next chapter.

Aircraft Handling, Servicing and Maintenance

Covered in this portion will be procedures for accomplishing the everyday operations. Such items as ground handling, the use of external power, moving and towing the copter, as well as parking, mooring and servicing. It also deals with the normal servicing operations, such as filling the fuel and oil system. Here's an example:

Replacing Transmission Lubrication Pump Oil Filter

1. Remove interior trim and blower access door.
2. Position container of cloth to catch residual oil. Loosen and remove filter housing by turning counterclockwise.
3. Remove filter element.
4. Inspect filter element for metal particles. If metal particles are present, remove main transmission chip detectors and inspect for other evidence of internal failure in the gearbox.
5. Install new filter element and new O-rings.
6. Install and tighten housing.

7. If necessary, replenish transmission oil supply, then perform ground runup of helicopter, and check split-line for oil leakage.
8. Reinstall, in order, blower access door and interior trim.

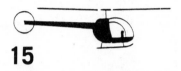

15

WEIGHT & BALANCE

All helicopters, like all aircraft, are designed for certain weight and balance conditions. But it's you, the PIC, who is responsible for making sure that the specified weight and balance limitations are met before takeoff. Any pilot who does takeoff in a helicopter that isn't within the designed weight and balance condition isn't only violating FAA regulations but is inviting disaster.

Four kinds of weight must be considered in the loading of every machine. They are empty weight, useful load, gross weight and maximum (allowable) gross weight.

Empty Weight can be described as the weight of the helicopter, including the structure, the powerplant, all fixed equipment, all fixed ballast, unusable fuel, undrainable oil and the total quantity of both engine coolant and hydraulic fluid.

Useful Load is the weight of the pilot, passengers, baggage (including removeable ballast) usable fuel and drainable oil.

Gross Weight is simply the empty weight plus the useful load. The sum of these two weights must now be compared with the fourth weight to be considered—maximum gross weight.

Maximum Gross Weight is the heaviest weight for which the craft is certificated to fly or operate under varying condi-

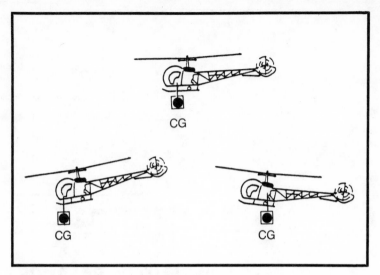

Notice the CG effect on cyclic position and helicopter attitude during hovering flight.

tions. Some helicopter manufacturers use the term "basic weight" in determining the weight and balance of their helicopters. Basic weight includes the empty weight, as previously defined, plus the weight of the drainable oil. Whenever the term "basic weight" is used, it should be understood that this is its meaning.

Although a helicopter is certificated for a specified maximum gross weight, it will not be safe to take off with this load under all situations. Conditions that affect takeoff, climb, hovering and landing performance may require the off-loading of fuel, passengers or baggage to a weight less than the maximum allowable. Such conditions would include high altitudes, high temperatures and high humidity, the combination of which makes for a high density altitude. Additional factors to consider are takeoff and landing surfaces, takeoff and landing distances and the presence of obstacles.

Because of the various adverse conditions that may exist, many times you'll have to decide the needs of the type of mission to be flown, and load your craft accordingly. For example, if all seats are occupied and maximum baggage is carried, gross weight limitations could dictate that less than max fuel be carried. On the other hand, if you're interested in

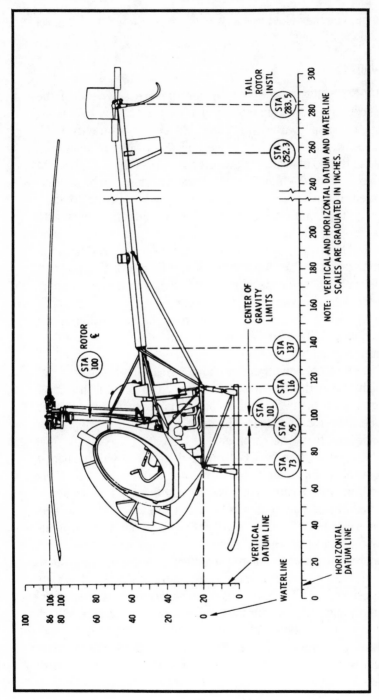

Balance Diagram.

range, you may elect to carry a full load but fewer passengers and less baggage.

Balance

Not only must you consider the gross weight of the helicopter, but you must also determine that the load is arranged to fall within the allowable center-of-gravity (CG) range, which is specified in the helicopter flight manual. The CG is the point where the copter is in balance—the point at which all the weight of the system is considered to be concentrated. If the helicopter were suspended by a string attached to the "CG Point," the craft's fuselage would remain parallel to the ground, much as a perfectly balanced teeter-totter. The allowable range in which the CG must fall is referred to as the "CG Range." The exact location and length of this range is specified for each machine, but it usually extends a short distance fore and aft of the main rotor mast. For most helicopter types, the location of the CG must be kept within much narrower limits than for airplanes—in some cases less than three inches.

The ideal condition is to have a machine in such perfect balance that the fuselage will remain horizontal in hovering flight, with no cyclic pitch control necessary, except that necessary for windage. The fuselage acts as a pendulum suspended from the rotor.

Any change in the CG changes the angle at which it hangs from this point of support. If the weight is concentrated directly under the rotor mast, the helicopter hangs horizontal; if the center-of-gravity is too far aft of the mast, the machine hangs with nose tilted up; and if the CG is too far forward of the mast, the nose tilts down. Hence, out of balance loading of the chopper makes control more difficult and decreases maneuverability, since cyclic travel is restricted in the direction opposite of the CG location. Because helicopters are relatively narrow and high sideward speeds will not be attained, lateral balance presents no problems in normal flight instruction and passenger flights, but some light helicopters specify the seat from which solo flight must be made. However, if external loads are carried in such a position that a large, lateral displacement of the cyclic is required to maintain level flight, fore and aft cyclic movements might be limited.

CG Forward Of Allowable Limits

This condition arises more often in two-place helicopters; a heavy pilot and passenger take off without baggage or proper ballast located aft of the rotor mast. The condition will become worse as the flight progresses, due to fuel consumption, if the main fuel tank is located behind the rotor mast.

You'll recognize this condition after coming to a hover, following a vertical takeoff. The copter will have a nose-low attitude, and an excessive rearward cyclic will be required to hold a hover in a no-wind condition, if hovering flight can be maintained at all. Flight under this condition shouldn't be

If new equipment is added or taken away from the helicopter after leaving manufacturer, it must be corrected on the craft's weight & balance. These two items could be enough to warrant a change.

continued, since the possibility of running out of rearward cyclic control will increase rapidly as fuel is consumed. You might even find it impossible to increase the pitch attitude sufficiently to bring the chopper to a stop. Also, in case of engine failure and the resulting autorotation, sufficient cyclic might not be available to flare properly for the landing.

Hovering in a strong wind will make a forward CG less easy to recognize, since less rearward displacement of the cyclic will be required than when hovering in a no-wind condition. You should, therefore, consider the wind speed in which you're hovering and its relation to the rearward displacement of the cyclic in determining if a critical balance condition exists.

CG Aft of Maximum Limits

Without proper ballast in the cockpit, this condition could arise when: a lightweight pilot takes off solo with a full load of fuel located aft of the rotor mast; a lightweight pilot takes off with maximum baggage allowed in a compartment located behind the rotor mast; or a lightweight pilot takes off with a combination of baggage and substantial fuel where both are aft of the rotor mast. You'll recognize this condition after bringing the craft to a hover, following a vertical takeoff. The chopper will have a tail-low attitude, and an excessive forward cyclic will be required to hold a hover in a no-wind condition, if a hover can be maintained at all. If there's a wind, an even greater forward displacement will be required.

If you continue flight in this condition, you could find it impossible to fly at high airspeeds due to insufficient forward cyclic displacement to hold a nose-low attitude. This particular condition could become quite dangerous if gusty or rough air accelerates the machine to a higher airspeed than forward cyclic will allow. The nose will start to rise and full forward cyclic might be insufficient to hold it down or lower it once it does rise.

Weight & Balance Information

When a helicopter is delivered from the factory, the empty weight, empty weight CG and useful load for each particular craft are noted on a weight & balance data sheet included in the helicopter flight manual. These quantities will vary for different helicopters of a given series, depending on variations in fixed equipment included in each helicopter when delivered.

If, after delivery, additional fixed equipment is added, or if some is removed, or a major repair or alteration is made which may affect the empty weight, empty weight CG or useful load, the weight and balance data must be revised to reflect this new information and its effect on that particular craft. All weight and balance changes will be entered in the appropriate aircraft records. This generally will be the aircraft logbook. Make sure you use the latest weight and balance data in computing all loading problems.

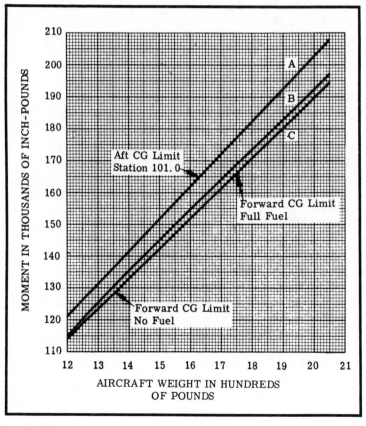

Loading Chart.

Sample Weight & Balance Problem

In loading a helicopter for flight you have to answer two very basic questions: Is its gross weight within the "maximum allowable gross weight," and does that weight's CG fall within the allowable "CG range?"

To answer the first question, merely add the weight of the items comprising the useful load (pilot, passengers, useable fuel, drainable oil and baggage) to the empty weight of the machine. Then check the total weight obtained to see that it doesn't exceed maximum allowable gross weight. If basic weight is used in computing weight and balance, then the weight of the oil is included with this weight.

To answer the second question, use the loading chart or loading table in the aircraft's flight manual for the particular helicopter being flown.

Sample Problem: Determine if the gross weight and CG are within allowable limits under the following conditions based on the sample loading charts.

	Pounds
Basic Weight	1070
Fuel (full tank—30 gallons)	180
Pilot (Station 83.2)	170
Passenger (right hand—Station 83.2)	170
Passenger (center—Station 80.0)	170

By adding the individual weights together, you should come out with a gross weight sum of 1760 pounds. Now, does the gross weight fall at or below the maximum allowable gross weight specified for this helicopter? With a maximum gross of 2050 pounds, 1760 gross is well below max.

How about CG range, does the "CG point" fall within the CG range? With the use of the "Load Weight—Pounds" chart, find the moment in thousands of inch-pounds for each position or station. With the sample, as stated above, it should look something like this:

	Pounds	Moment
Basic Weight	1070	108,915
Fuel (full tank—30 gallons)	180	19,260
Pilot (Station 83.2)	170	14,144
Passenger (right hand—Station 83.2)	170	14,144
Passenger (center—Station 80.0)	170	13,600
	1760	170,063

Where will the total moment and weight fall within the CG Range? To find out, simply go to the loading chart and plot the CG. First, plot the aircraft's gross weight in hundreds of pounds across the bottom of the chart, and the total moment in thousands of inch-pounds vertically on the left side. Once these two points have been found, it's simply a matter of drawing a line vertically up the chart from pounds and a line horizontally across the chart from the moment. Where these two intersect on the chart will be your craft's CG point. Does this CG point fall within the CG range (the bold, black lines)? Sure it does. It's between lines "A" and "B" and, therefore, your loading meets all balance requirements.

Sample problems such as this should be worked until you feel comfortable using the craft's charts and graphs. It also makes you more familiar with the operation of your particular helicopter, and this means a safer operation.

GLOSSARY

GLOSSARY

advancing blade: As the rotor spins around its shaft, the blade turning into the wind is the advancing blade. If the helicopter is moving forward, the advancing blade will be in the right half of the rotor disc; if moving backward, it will be in the left; if moving sideward to the left, it will be in the forward half; and if moving sideward to the right, it will be in the rear half.

airfoil: Any surface designed to obtain a useful reaction from the air through which it moves in the form of lift. A streamline shape of aerodynamic surfaces which are designed to produce a minimum of drag and a maximum of lift.

angle of attack: The acute angle measured between the chord of an airfoil and the relative wind.

articulated rotor: A rotor system in which the blades are free to flap, drag and feather. A mode of attaching the rotor blade to the mast. A blade is said to be "fully articulated" when it's similar to the shoulder joint in its root attachment. This joint allows the rotor blade to flap up and down, move fore and aft to lead and lag and twist around its own axis in a feathering motion.

autorotation: Self-energized turning of the rotor. Unlike "windmilling," where blade pitch is negative and energy is extracted from the rotor, autorotation is obtained with slightly positive pitch settings and no energy is extracted from the rotor. This creates maximum amount of lift.

bank: Sideward tilt of. It may be necessary to keep the craft from skidding, or side-slipping, during a turn. In a correctly executed turn, the bank compensates for the centrifugal force, and the pilot is pressed straight down into the seat, without any side force.

blade: One of the blades of the rotor. Usually more than just one is used. If the rotor has two or three or more blades, it's described as a two-bladed or three-bladed rotor, respectively.

blade damper: A device; spring, friction or hydraulic, installed on the vertical (drag) hinge to diminish or dampen blade oscillation (hunting) around this hinge.

blade loading: The load placed on the rotor blades of a helicopter, determined by dividing the gross weight of the copter by the combined area of all rotor blades.

camber: Is the curvature of the centerline of an airfoil. A symmetrical airfoil is said to have zero camber, because its mean contour is flat and the upper surface of the airfoil is a mirror image of the bottom surface.

ceiling: Maximum height to which a given helicopter can climb. Air is thinner at higher altitudes and the ceiling is reached when either the engine loses too much power or the blade airfoil begins to stall, or both. This happens at "absolute ceiling." An altitude at which the craft still has the ability to climb 100 fpm is "service ceiling."

center of gravity (CG): An imaginary point where the resultant of all weight forces in the body may be considered to be concentrated for any position of the body.

center of pressure: The imaginary point on the chord line of an airfoil where the resultant of all aerodynamic forces of the airfoil section may be considered to be concentrated.

centrifugal force: The force created by the tendency of a body to follow a straight-line path against the force which causes it to move in a curve, resulting in a force which tends to pull away from the axis of rotation. Applied to the helicopter, the force that would make the rotor blade fly out if it were not attached at the hub.

chord: The length of an airfoil as depicted by an imaginary straight line between the leading and trailing edges of that airfoil.

chordwise balance: An engineering term that refers to the mass balance of the airfoil. It's usually made to coincide with its center of lift. If this is not done, blade flutter could develop in flight, which might destroy the entire blade.

collective pitch control (collective): Affecting all rotor blades in the same way. Collective pitch control changes the pitch of all rotor blades in unison, thus varying the total lift of the rotor. The method of control by which the pitch of all rotor blades is varied equally and simultaneously.

cone angle (coning angle): The angle a rotor blade makes with the plane of rotation, similar to the dihedral angle of a fixed wing. Since the rotor blade is hinged at the hub, it's held out by centrifugal force, but since it also produces lift, it's deflected upward.

coriolis effect: The tendency of a mass to increase or decrease its angular velocity, when its radius of rotation is shortened or lengthened, respectively.

cyclic pitch control: Repetitive once-around-the-circle change in the pitch angle of each rotor blade as it turns around the axis. Cyclic control is also known as "azimuth" control, and its purpose is to tilt the direction of lift force of the rotor, rather than to change its magnitude. The control which changes the pitch of the rotor blades individually during a cycle of revolution to control the tilt of the rotor disc and, therefore, the direction and velocity of horizontal flight.

delta hinge (flapping hinge): The hinge with its axis parallel to the rotor plane of rotation, which permits the rotor blades to flap to equalize lift between the rotor disc.

damper: A mechanical device, similar to a shock absorber, installed on helicopters for the purpose of preventing the buildup of destructive oscillations. Dampers are found in rotorcraft in two critical areas: on the landing gear and on lag hinges of rotor blades. Without dampers, dangerous "ground resonance" would occur on many modern copters.

density altitude: Pressure altitude corrected for temperature and humidity. An altitude that's computed from the three H's (high altitude, high temperature and high humidity). Your craft performs like it's at that altitude, even though it's actually at a different altitude MSL.

disc: An area swept by the rotor blades. Although the rotor in flight actually sweeps a cone surface, for purposes of calculations, it's customary to speak of it as a disc. This is a circle, with its center at the hub axis and a radius of one blade length.

disc loading: Is similar to "wing loading" of a fixed winger. It's the ratio of helicopter gross weight to rotor disc area (total chopper weight divided by the rotor disc area). The greater the disc loading the greater is the craft's sinking speed with power off and the steeper its angle of glide. Most helicopters are disc-loaded three to five, but some heavy cargo copters' disc loading goes up to 10.

dissymmetry of lift: The unequal lift across the rotor disc resulting from the difference in the velocity of air over the advancing blade half and retreating blade half of the rotor disc area.

fatigue: A property of structural materials, similar to that of human beings, which makes them break down under repeated stresses, while they wouldn't break down under stresses twice as high if applied only a few times. Vibration is the major cause of fatigue failures in helicopters. Because vibration cannot be completely eliminated from rotorcraft, fatigue is still the number one enemy of its designers and also the user.

feathering axis: The axis about which the pitch angle of a rotor blade is varied. Sometimes referred to as spanwise axis. Rotating around the long axis of the rotor blade, changing its pitch angle. In helicopters, feathering axis usually is designed to go through the quarter-chord of the airfoil to minimize control stick forces.

feathering action: That action which changes the pitch angle of the rotor blades periodically, by rotating them around their feathering (spanwise) axis.

flapping: The vertical movement of a blade about a delta (flapping) hinge. Rotor blades flap as much as eight degrees in forward flight. Without flapping, a craft would roll over on its side, because the advancing blade would produce more lift than the retreating blade.

flare (flareout): A landing maneuver in which the angle of attack is increased near the ground; executed in helicopters as well as fixed wing craft and birds, which consumes the kinetic energy of forward velocity to arrest the descent. In a correctly executed flareout, horizontal velocity and vertical velocity come to zero at the same time, making a perfect zero-speed touchdown.

flutter: A self-induced oscillating motion of an aerodynamic surface, such as the main or tail rotors. It resembles, somewhat, the flapping motion of a bird's wings, except that energy is extracted from the airstream rather than pumped into it. Noseweights on rotor blades are installed to prevent flutter. Occurences of flutter in copters can be catastrophic and must be avoided at all costs.

freewheeling unit: A component part of the transmission or power train which automatically disconnects the main rotor from the engine when the engine stops or slows below the equivalent of rpm.

gimbal: A mechanism which permits the tilt of the rotor head in any direction, but restrains its rotation. If axes of tilt don't intersect the axis of rotation of a rotor, the gimbal is said to be "offset." A correctly designed Offset Gimball Head allows the craft to fly hands-off for an unlimited length of time.

ground effect: The "cushion" of denser air confined beneath the rotor system of a hovering helicopter, which gives additional lift and, thus, decreases the power required to hover. It's the extra buoyancy near the ground, which makes the craft float a few feet off the ground on a pillow of air. Ground proximity does, in fact, increase the lift of a rotor up to the height of one diameter above the surface.

ground resonance: A violent "dance jig" that a helicopter sometimes develops when its rotor is turning while it stands on the ground. It happens only to choppers equipped with lag hinges and inadequate dampers. Lag motions of the blades become amplified by the flexibility of the landing gear, and the craft can destroy itself in a few seconds, if power is not shut off at once.

gyroscopic precession: A characteristic of all rotating bodies. When a force is applied to the periphery of a rotating body parallel to its axis of rotation, the rotating body will tilt in the direction of the applied force 90 degrees later in the plane of rotation.

hovering in ground effect (HIGE): Maintaining a fixed position over a spot on the ground or water which compresses a cushion of high-density air between the main rotor and the ground or water surface and, thus, increases the lift produced by the main rotor. Normally, the main rotor must be within one-half rotor diameter to the ground or water surface in order to produce an efficient ground effect.

hovering out of ground effect (HOGE): Maintaining a fixed position over a spot on the ground or water at some altitude above the ground at which no additional lift is obtained from ground effect.

hunting: The tendency of a blade, due to coriolis effect, to seek a position ahead of, or behind, that which would be determined by centrifugal force alone.

lag-lead: Motions of blades in the plane of the rotor around "lag hinges." They were introduced on rotors with three or more blades to minimize severe, in-plane stresses caused by the difference in drag on the blade as it went from advancing to retreating positions. Not all rotors have lag hinges, some two-bladed rotors don't have them. They obtain the same lag-lead stress relief by using a flexible mast.

life: Maximum safe duration of operation of any part of a helicopter. It is limited by the probability of either fatigue failure or excessive wear. Life of ball bearings could be 10,000 hours; V-belts 500, rotor blades 2000 hours, etc. Everything on a helicopter must be regarded as having limited life of uncertain duration, unless designed by qualified, professional engineers for unlimited life.

milking: A term applied to a procedure for regaining main rotor rpm.

mast: Main structural member of the rotor craft which connects the airframe to the rotor. In spite of its simple function, the mast must be very carefully designed to minimize the feedback of damaging vibrations between the rotor and the airframe.

noseweight: A lead weight attached to the leading edge of an airfoil. Its function is to prevent flutter.

pattern: In-plane lineup of rotor blades so they perfectly balance each other. For example, in a two-bladed rotor, if the line connecting the center of gravity of each blade doesn't pass through the center of rotation, the blades are said to be "out of pattern." Such a rotor would develop a one-per-rev vibration similar to out-of-balance.

pitch angle: The angle between the chord line of a rotor blade and the reference plane of the main rotor hub or the rotor plane of rotation.

radius of action: Maximum distance a helicopter can fly from its home base and return, without refueling.

range: Maximum distance a helicopter can fly without landing or refueling.

redundancy: A fail-safe design which provides a second standby structural member should the main one fail, or providing two members to do the same function. Dual ignition in aircraft engines is a typical redundancy. Because doubling up of everything would be expensive in both the weight and money, engineers use redundancy only in those areas where the probability of failure of a single member is high, or where it would result in catastrophic damage.

retreating: Retreating blade is on the opposite side of the advancing blade. It travels with the wind created by the forward motion. If forward velocity of the craft is zero, and there is no wind, simply opposite the advancing blade.

rigid rotor: A rotor system with blades fixed to the hub in such a way that they can feather but cannot flap or drag.

roll: Tilt of the rotorcraft around its longitudinal axis. Controlled by lateral movements of the cyclic.

rotor: The lift-producing, rotarywing part of the rotorcraft. It consists of one or more blades and is correctly described as a two-bladed rotor, three-bladed rotor, etc. "Rotor blade" refers to a single blade only.

semirigid rotor: A rotor system in which the blades are fixed to the hub but are free to flap and to feather.

slip: The controlled flight of a helicopter in a direction not in line with its fore and aft axis.

solidity ratio: Portion of the rotor disc which is filled by rotor blades; a ratio of total blade area to the disc area. The ratio of total rotor blade area to total rotor disc area.

spar: The main, load-carrying, structural member of the rotor blade. It carries the centrifugal force as well as lift loads from the blade tip to the root attachment. A second spar sometimes is added for redundancy.

standard atmosphere: Atmospheric conditions in which the air is a dry, perfect gas; the temperature at sea level is 59 degrees F (15 degrees C); the pressure at sea level (or reduced to sea level) is 29.92 inches Hg; and the temperature gradient is about 3.5 degrees F per 1000-feet change in altitude.

swashplate: A tilting plate, mounted concentrically with the rotor shaft. It consists of rotating and non-rotating halves, the rotating part being connected to the pitch horns of each rotor blade, and the non-rotating part to the cyclic. Thus the pilot can control the pitch of each blade while the rotor is turning.

teetering: Hinge and motion around it, in see-saw fashion, in two-bladed rotors. It allows one blade to flap up and forces the other blade to flap down. Use of teetering hinge allows direct transfer of centrifugal forces from one blade to the other, without going through the mast and separate flapping hinges.

tip path: The plane in which rotor blade tips travel when rotating.

tip speed: Airspeed at the tip of the rotor blade. Too high a tip speed is wasteful in power, too low a tip speed gives problems of controlling the retreating blade. Tip speed of small rotorcraft varies from 300 fps (200 mph) to 750 fps (500 mph). Lower tip speed yields greater lifting efficiency.

tip stall: The stall condition on the retreating blade which occurs at high forward speeds.

torque: A force, or combination of forces, that tends to produce a countering rotating motion. In a single rotor helicopter, where the rotor turns counterclockwise, the fuselage tends to rotate clockwise (looking down on the helicopter). Anything that rotates and consumes power, produces a reaction torque in the direction opposite to its rotation. Tail (antitorque) rotors are added to helicopters to overcome torque produced by main rotor rotation.

tracking: Tracking of the rotor is an operation necessary to assure that every blade rotates in the same orbit. This means that each blade tip must follow the path of the preceeding one. If not, a vibration will develop, which is similar to the dynamic unbalance of a wheel. To put a rotor "in track," the trim tab of the low blade should be bent up and vice-versa.

transition: A narrow region of flight speed in helicopters, usually between 10-20 mph, when they slide off the ground cushion, and before they pick up the added lift of forward translation. The airflow pattern through the rotor changes erratically during transition and is often accompanied by roughness and partial loss of lift.

translational lift: The additional lift obtained through airspeed because of increased efficiency of the rotor system, whether when transitioning from a hover into horizontal flight or when hovering in a high wind.

trim tab: A small metal plate projecting behind the trailing edge, near the tip, of a rotor blade. Its purpose is to aid in "tracking" the rotor. Without trim tabs, the pitch of the entire rotor blade would have to be changed to adjust its track.

weave: A form of rotor-blade instability, which may be caused by excessive, elastic softness of the rotor blade or of the control system. When weave occurs in improperly designed craft, the rotor suddenly stops following the pilot's commands and darts, seemingly, out of control. Like flutter, it must not be permitted to occur in flight.

yaw: Turning of the helicopter right or left around its vertical axis. In helicopters, its done by changing the pitch of the tail rotor.

INDEX

A

Aircraft handling, servicing &
   maintenance 179
Air density & lift 37
Airflow, transverse 52
Airfoil 31
Allowable limits 184
Angle, blade pitch 33
Angle of attack 33
Antitorque pedals 59
Approach 113
Approach, normal 116
   steep 118
Autorotation 125
Autorotation, hovering 128
   no flare 130
Auxiliary rotors 45
Axis of rotation 49

B

Balance 183
Blade flapping 48
Blade pitch angle 33
Blade stall 144

C

Carburetor icing 165
Climb, normal 108
Clutch 68
Confined area operations 156

Coning / D / E / F column

Coning 48
Coriolis effect 49
Cyclic pitch control 63

D

Descent, normal 110
Drag 39

E

Emergency & malfunction
   procedures 173
Engine failure 147
Engine start procedures 173
Extreme attitudes &
   overcontrolling 162

F

Flight, forward 42
   hovering 41
   hovering sideward 99
Flight manual, helicopter 169
Flight, sideward 42
   straight & level 103
Flight techniques 163
Flight, vertical 41
Forward flight 42
Forward flight, hovering 96
Freewheeling unit 70

G

Ground effect	51
Gyroscopic precession	46

H

Helicopter flight manual	169
High altitude pilot technique	163
High frequency vibrations	151
Hovering	91
Hovering autorotation	128
Hovering flight	41
Hovering forward flight	96
Hovering rearward flight	101
Hovering sideward flight	99
Hovering turn	92
Hover to hover	98

I

Icing, carburetor	165
Instrument readings	166

L

Landing	113, 121
Lift	34, 47
Lift, translational	52
Low frequency vibrations	150
Low rotor RPM	143

M

Maximum limits	186
Maximum performance takeoff	86
Medium frequency vibrations	151

N

No flare autorotation	130
Normal approach	116
Normal climb	108
Normal descent	110
Normal procedures	173
Normal takeoff	82

O

Operations, confined area	156
slope	153
Operating limits, Rotor RPM	162

P

Pedals, antitorque	59
Pendular action	53
Pitch control	55
Power recovery	133

R

Reading, instrument	166
Rearward flight, hovering	101
Rotary-wing history	7
Rotation, axis	49
Rotor RPM operating limits	162
Rotors, auxiliary	45
Rotor system	72
RPM, low rotor	143
Running takeoff	84

S

Shallow approach & running landing	122
Sideward flight	42
Slope operations	153
Stall	39
Steep approach	118
Straight & level flight	103
S-turns	135
Swash plate assembly	70

T

Tail rotor control system failure	148
Takeoff, maximum performance	86
normal	82
running	84
vertical	80
Tall grass & water operations	164
Throttle control	58
Thrust	38
Torque	45
Translating tendency (drift)	51
Translational lift	52
Transmission system	67
Transverse airflow	52
Tree topper	141
Turns	106

V

Vertical flight	41
Vertical takeoff	80
Vibrations, high frequency	151
low frequency	150
medium frequency	151
Vortex ring condition	146

W

Weight	40, 181
Weight & balance	179
Weight & balance information	186
Wind, relative	32